WHY DOES MAN SUFFER?

BIBLICAL PERSPECTIVE

LESLIE M. JOHN

WHY DOES MAN SUFFER

BIBLICAL PERSPECTIVE

LESLIE M. JOHN

DESCRIPTION

This book is based on the teachings of the Bible. Among several important teachings, the teaching on suffering is vividly laid out in the New Testament.

Suffering started in the Garden of Eden, when man transgressed God's command, and the man and the woman were cast out of the Garden, and lost fellowship with God.

Man has choice to live for God transforming his old nature and becoming a new creature in the Lord, or choose to live lewd and vulgar life. The consequences of living outside the purview of the teachings of the Bible are very serious.

Unless man chooses to have right thinking and live a good and pleasing life he would end up in suffering. Suffering may be either of physical, or of mental, but living a sinful life will surely lead to suffering.

Bible admonishes to rejoice when suffering overtakes us for right reasons. It is such suffering that causes man to come closer to God.

Because God is love, He sent His one and only Son, Lord Jesus Christ into this world to save mankind from perishing and to reconcile them to the Father. When Man suffers from either pain, loss, or sickness, he will no longer have inclination to sin anymore. Suffering overtakes man's capacity of sinning.

Lord Jesus said...

"Blessed are they which are persecuted for righteousness' sake: for theirs is the kingdom of heaven". (Matthew 5:10)

Suffering for the right cause brings blessings, while suffering for wrong reasons brings disaster in life. There is a great difference between suffering for the right cause and suffering for criminal activities. Suffering for illegal causes and feeling sorry over such actions would not absolve one from being punished in this world, or in the world to come.

ABOUT THE AUTHOR

The author, who accepted Lord Jesus Christ as his personal Savior when he was a boy of 13, was raised in a Christian family and had education in Christian Institutions.

This then was the message that he heard of the Son of God, Lord Jesus Christ. This then is the message that he declares that God is light and in Him there is no darkness at all. Jesus Christ is the Son of God sent from above to save sinners.

Jesus died on the cross bearing our sins upon Himself. He was buried and God raised Him on the third day. Jesus, after having appeared to many for 40 days ascended to heaven. He will come again. Whosoever confesses his/her sins to Him and believe in heart that God raised Him from the dead will not perish but will have everlasting life.

"Jesus saith unto him, I am the way, the truth, and the life: no man cometh unto the Father, but by me" (John 14:6).

SCRIPTURES

Scriptures quoted in this book are from KJV from open domain, and from NIV, ESV, and NLT not greater than the number permitted.

ISBN-13: 978-0-9985181-3-8
ISBN-10: 0-9985181-3-1

Table of Contents

SECTION I

SUFFERING CAUSES TO CEASE FROM SIN

CHAPTER 1

SUFFERING, CAUSES AND

CONSEQUENCES

THE BEGINNING OF THE SUFFERING

The suffering of mankind started with Adam the first man on this earth transgressing God's command in the Garden of Eden, where the LORD said to him that he can freely eat of every tree of the garden, but of the tree of the knowledge of good and evil he should not eat. There was a consequence attached to that command, and that was on the day that he eats of the tree the tree of knowledge and evil he will surely die.

"And the LORD God commanded the man, saying, of every tree of the garden thou may freely eat: But of the tree of the knowledge of good and evil, thou shalt not eat of it: for in the day that thou eat thereof thou shalt surely die" (Genesis 2:16-17)

The LORD God caused a deep sleep upon Adam and while he was sleeping God took one of the ribs of the man and made a woman out of the rib and brought to him. Adam called her as "Woman" because she was taken out of Man. God said to the man to be fruitful, multiply, replenish the earth, and subdue it and have dominion over the fish of the sea, fowl of the air and every living thing that moves on the earth. (Genesis 2:8-28).

SATAN DECEIVED MAN

The serpent, who was more subtle than any other beast of the field, deceived the woman with his enticing words. The serpent spoke to her and convinced her that God did not tell the truth. The woman yielded to the temptation of the serpent. She saw that the tree was good for food and pleasure for the eyes and thought the tree would give her intelligence. She took of its fruit and ate and also gave to her husband and he ate it.

The eyes of both of them opened and they knew that they were naked. They made aprons for themselves with fig-leaves and when they heard the voice of God, whose name is "Jehovah Elohim" they hid themselves from his presence. Jehovah Elohim called man and asked him where he was?

The man said he feared because he was naked and hid himself. God demanded an answer from the man as to who said to him that he was naked and questioned if he had he eaten fruit of the tree that he was asked not to eat from! The man blamed woman and the woman blamed the serpent.

THE CURSE FROM GOD

The LORD God cursed the earth for man; the woman with pain in her child labor, and God cursed serpent that the serpent would crawl all the days of his life. This resulted in Adam toiling for food; woman who was in Adam and who became his wife to be a help-mate was cursed with pain in her child-bearing.

The serpent who was not crawling before became a most loathed reptile on the earth to crawl on the earth his entire life. God put enmity between the seed of the woman and of the serpent. Adam called the woman as "Eve" because she was the mother of all living. This is how the sin entered the world. In order to reconcile man to God, Jesus relinquished his glory in heaven and came down into this world in the form of man and lived among us.

There is no dearth of people in the world, suffering pain and sickness as a consequence of their willful acts of committing sin. Some, who have enjoyed pleasures of the world, get enlightened after watching others suffer. They make known to others their learning about suffering. Those, who are learning from the errors eventually teach others to be careful.

CHAPTER 2

SIN IN ITSELF IS A DISEASE

When a man sins, he is embracing disease. On accepting Lord Jesus as savior, sinner's soul is redeemed, and upon confession that Jesus is Lord and believing in heart that God raised Him from the dead, he/she will surely be in heaven (Rom.10:9-10); but his physical body will be redeemed only on resurrection.

David decries his condition after sinning!

References:

Psalm 38:3-22 – David decries his condition

2 Samuel 12:15-23 — David lost his child in spite praying ardently. God does everything according to His purposes.

Psalm 42:11 — David decries on his soul cast down

"There is no soundness in my flesh because of thine anger; neither is there any rest in my bones because of my sin. For mine iniquities are gone over mine head: as a heavy burden they are too heavy for me. My wounds stink and are corrupt because of my foolishness. I am troubled; I am bowed down greatly; I go mourning all the day long. For my loins are filled with a loathsome disease: and there is no soundness in my flesh. I am feeble and sore broken: I have roared by reason of the disquietness of my heart. Lord, all my desire is before thee; and my groaning is not hid from thee. My heart panteth, my strength faileth me: as for the light of mine eyes, it also is gone from me. My lovers and my friends stand aloof from my sore;

and my kinsmen stand afar off. They also that seek after my life lay snares for me: and they that seek my hurt speak mischievous things, and imagine deceits all the day long. But I, as a deaf man, heard not; and I was as a dumb man that openeth not his mouth. Thus I was as a man that heareth not, and in whose mouth are no reproofs. For in thee, O LORD, do I hope: thou wilt hear, O Lord my God. For I said, hear me, lest otherwise they should rejoice over me: when my foot slips, they magnify themselves against me. For I am ready to halt, and my sorrow is continually before me. For I will declare mine iniquity; I will be sorry for my sin. But mine enemies are lively, and they are strong: and they that hate me wrongfully are multiplied. They also that render evil for good are mine adversaries; because I follow the thing that good is. Forsake me not, O LORD: O my God, be not far from me. Make haste to help me, O Lord my salvation" (Psalms 38:3-22)

YIELDING TO TEMPTATION

"No temptation has overtaken you except what is common to mankind. And God is faithful; he will not let you be tempted beyond what you can bear. But when you are tempted, he will also provide a way out so that you can endure it" (1 Corinthians 10:13)

Usually a saved child of God complains that he could not endure Satan's temptation, and therefore, he committed a sin. Often he would quote that "no man is perfect" and then keeps sinning even after being born-again. If we strictly consider the teachings of John, it is evident that a man of God would not keep on committing sin.

Transgression of law is sin, and continual sinning is tantamount to practicing lawlessness. Lord Jesus, who is incarnate God, came down to this earth to take away sins. Whoever is born-again abides in the Lord, and the Lord in him; but if a born-again child of God keeps on sinning it is certain that he has neither seen Him nor known Him.

"Everyone who makes a practice of sinning also practices lawlessness; sin is lawlessness. You know that he appeared in order to take away sins, and in him there is no sin. No one who abides in him keeps on sinning; no one who keeps on sinning has either seen him or known him" 1 John 3:4-6

The scripture says no temptation is beyond the controlling power of a believer. Every temptation a believer faces is common to mankind. God is faithful and He does not allow a believer to be tempted beyond his capacity of tolerance can bear. In fact, when a believer is tempted God shows a way out to escape from yielding to temptation so that a believer can endure it, and overcome it. If a believer still falls into sin, thereafter, it is his fault, and is surely because he has opted to fall into it voluntarily.

In spite of provision for escapement route the Lord provided, if a believer still falls into sin and seeks forgiveness from God, the Lord is faithful to forgive his sin.

"If we say we have no sin, we deceive ourselves, and the truth is not in us. If we confess our sins, he is faithful and just to forgive us our sins and to cleanse us from all unrighteousness. If we say we have not sinned, we make him a liar, and his word is not in us" (1 John 1:8-10)

The Lord is compassionate and long-suffering and that is the reason why He is continuously interceding on behalf of believers in Christ sitting at the right hand of the Majesty. There is no strength in the argument that a believer will never sin after being born-again. As long as we are in flesh made of dust, we are fallible. Yet, there is consolation in the Scriptures that no temptation from Satan is greater than our capacity to bear.

"He is the radiance of the glory of God and the exact imprint of his nature, and he upholds the universe by the word of his power. After making purification for sins, he sat down at the right hand of the Majesty on high (Hebrews 1:3 ESV)

"Consequently, he is able to save to the uttermost those who draw near to God through him, since he always lives to make intercession for them. (Hebrews 7:25 ESV)

CHAPTER 3

LEWD AND VULGAR LIFE

Suffering controls man and his attitude. Not everyone, who suffers pain, would think of committing sin again. The suffering in most cases is because of indulging in sin. The man, who commits sin suffers pain, and diseases, in most cases with serious diseases. Not only he would pay penalty in his body, but he would spend much of his time seeing doctors, and in some cases paying alimony.

However, there are two different kinds of suffering a man could face in his life. One, it is choosing to live in debauchery, revelry, partying, etc. The revelry and partying may appear to be pleasant and happy in most cases, but in the long run, they are harmful financially, mentally and physically. Any behavior, which exceeds moderate limits is harmful.

Simon Peter, the disciple of Jesus Christ advises us to arm ourselves with spiritual warfare just as Lord Jesus Christ armed Himself, and suffered for our sake. Lord Jesus Christ, who was sinless, made Himself to be sin for us taking upon Himself our sin in order to provide us the way for salvation (cf. 2 Corinthians 5:21). However, man is saved only if he confesses his sin to Him and requests for forgiveness, in addition to accepting Jesus as Lord and by believing in heart that God raised Him from the dead on the third day.

While choosing to live for God man needs to transform to adhere to the teachings of Lord Jesus Christ, and be cross-bearer for the sake of our Lord. Bible says one may persecute a believer in Christ, and may even kill him, but in doing so, one would be able to put an end to the physical body of the believer, and never the soul of the believer.

The word of God says to fear the Lord, who has the authority not only to kill the body but the soul as well, and such a one is none other than the Lord Himself. One, who chooses live a life of lewd and vulgar life, is like pig living in cesspool. They find happiness in the cesspool, and would invite others also to enjoy dirt in the cesspool.

A believer in Christ should never yield to the temptation of Satan, who would mold a sinner to drown in the dirty cesspool of sin, and lead him to be cast into 'lake of fire' along with him. It is a place where there is no end of gnashing of teeth, and the thirst that never quenches.

A man, who suffers in body ceases committing sin, because he cannot bear the pain, and in his pain, he would call God to help him out of suffering.

The consequences of committing sin are great and the suffering that follows the sin would be so intense in man hat he would not live any longer in lusts of men, but to the will of God.

Bible admonishes us not to live the way worldly people do, and avoid walking in lewd, vulgar behavior, drinking excess of wine, indulging in revelry, banqueting, and abominable idolatry.

A born-again believer in Christ would face ridicule from the group of worldly people, when he withdraws from them, who indulged in worldly activities, and may even has to suffer when they speak evil against him.

However, the Word of God encourages believer that they, who despise him will face one day the Lord, who judges the quick and the dead. This is the reason why the Gospel is preached to everyone in order that they may accept Jesus as their personal savior, but if they reject Him as their personal savior, they are responsible for their rejection of salvation, and therefore, they will be judged according to their deeds in flesh. There is everlasting life and to live in the spirit for all those who accept Jesus Christ as their personal savior.

1 Peter 4:6 is often misinterpreted that the Gospel of Jesus Christ is preached to the dead and a second chance is given to them to be saved; nay, it does not say so. It says that Gospel of Jesus Christ was preached already to all those who are dead now, and all those who had accepted Jesus Christ as their personal savior before their death are saved and will rise from the dead in spirit with glorified bodies to be with the Lord forever and ever. (cf. 1 Thess. 4:16-17)

"For the Lord himself shall descend from heaven with a shout, with the voice of the archangel, and with the trump of God: and the dead in Christ shall rise first: Then we which are alive and remain shall be caught up together with them in the clouds, to meet the Lord in the air: and so shall we ever be with the Lord" (1 Thessalonians 4:16-17)

The Bible shows in 1 Peter 4:1-6 five important points to follow.

- Correct thinking in order to lead a correct living
- Choose suffering in order to live for God
- Avoid lustful thoughts
- Avoid the desire to retaliate
- Embrace the Gospel of Jesus Christ in order to lead victorious life.

CHAPTER 4

SUFFERER IN FLESH CEASES FROM SIN

"Forasmuch then as Christ hath suffered for us in the flesh, arm yourselves likewise with the same mind: for he that hath suffered in the flesh hath ceased from sin" (1 Peter 4:1)

Suffering is to feel pain or distress or to sustain injury or loss or undergo punishment such as 'death'.

Everyone in the world suffers from some kind of pain some time or whole time in one's life time. There is no exception. Adam sinned and lost his fellowship with God, and everyone, thereafter, is imputed with sin. Bible says, all have sinned and come short of the glory of God, and the wages of sin is death; but the gift of God is eternal life, through Jesus Christ, our Lord.

Man chooses either to live pure life transforming from his old nature or chooses to live lewd and vulgar life. Unless man chooses to have right thinking and live a good and pleasing life he would end up in suffering. Suffering may be either of physical, or of mental, but living a sinful life will surely lead to suffering.

Bible says everyone in the world has sinned and come short of the glory of God, and the wages of sin is death. If anyone says that he has not sinned in his life, he makes God a liar. However, God has given man provision to come out of that cesspool of sin, and live a pure life.

Man does not need to go the peak of a great mountain and practice aesthetics, or lead a secluded life to get a good and pleasing life, nor does he need to keep meditating at the foot of any tree. All that he has to do is to come to God and surrender his life Him allowing Him to lead his life.

It is as simple as accepting Lord Jesus Christ as one's personal savior, and believing in heart that God raised Him from the dead on the third day. Lord Jesus Christ died on behalf of us bearing our sin and shame, and therefore, we do not need to spend our energy to secure salvation (cf. Romans 3:23; 6:23; Romans 10:9-10; 1 John 1:8-10; John 3:16)

The only way to receive salvation, which is a free gift from God, is to repent of sins, confess that Jesus is Lord, and believe in heart that God raised Him from the dead on the third day. Lord Jesus Christ is incarnate God, who came down in the form of a servant and in the likeness of man, in fulfilment of the Father's will, to die on behalf of sinners.

Jesus Christ shed His precious blood on the cross, and whosoever accepts Him as his/her personal savior, will receive everlasting life, which is a promise from the Lord. He had humbled to the level of man, and offered His body and blood for the sake of reconciling man to God. He suffered on the cross. He bore crown of thorns on his head, and suffered scourging on our behalf. His palms and feet were nailed to the cross, and bled on our behalf.

There were no thorns in the beginning in God's creation, but man by his disobedience to God, brought curse upon the ground, which produced thorns and thistles. Lord Jesus took that curse upon Himself, in order that we may not bear that curse.

Lord Jesus bore our sin and shame on behalf of us, in order that we, by accepting Him as savior, receive salvation. He was raised from the dead on the third day in glorified body. He was raised in flesh and not as a spiritual being. He showed Himself not only to his disciple, Thomas Didymus, who doubted, but to many. The Lord said to Thomas to feel His palms that were nailed to the cross, and thrust his hand into the Lord's side. He did as the Lord said, and was convinced that the Lord was Jesus Christ.

"Then saith he to Thomas, Reach hither thy finger, and behold my hands; and reach hither thy hand, and thrust it into my side: and be not faithless, but believing" (John 20:27)

"Jesus saith unto him, Thomas, because thou hast seen me, thou hast believed: blessed are they that have not seen, and yet have believed" (John 20:29)

Lord Jesus Christ allowed Thomas to feel his palms and see the nail marks and said blessed are they that have not seen and yet have believed. Lord Jesus Christ, appeared not only to his disciples, but also to many while He was on earthly mission. After His resurrection from the dead He was on this earth for forty days appearing to several people that they may believe that He is Lord Jesus Christ, indeed, who rose from the dead.

After finishing His earthly mission the Lord ascended into heaven in the presence of His disciples and several people. He is now seated on the right hand of God. All angels, and authorities are made subject to Lord Jesus Christ. (cf. 1 Peter 3:21-22; Hebrews 1:3; Matthew 28:18; Luke 24:51; Acts 1:9)

When a person accepts Jesus as his/her personal savior, he/she is cleansed of all her sin and he/she is ceased from his/her sin, and sin cannot have dominion over a believer in Christ. Apostle Paul, Peter, and John all alike say that a truly born again child will not become a victim of sin again.

Nevertheless, as man lives in this world, he may come across several situations in day-to-day life, where he would break the commandments of God and is defiled, but that is not without any solution. God says "If we confess our sins, he is faithful and just to forgive us our sins, and to cleanse us from all unrighteousness" (1 John 1:9).

One thing a man should bear in mind is that no temptation from Satan is greater than he can bear with the help of God. Surely God provides a way out from the temptation, and from sinning, if a man falls into sin in spite of the provisions God makes for him/her to escape from committing sin, then he is responsible for his sin.

There is a consequence attached to every kind of sin a man commits, and when a man suffers the consequence, which is painful, he calls upon God, to forgive his sins. God is not unfaithful not to forgive his sins, but He will surely forgive his sins.

The question is how many times God would forgive? Lord Jesus Christ Himself answered a similar question from Peter once, and said we should forgive our enemies seven times seventy times. If that be the case, Almighty God, who is compassionate, and long-suffering will surely forgive our sins as many times or even more than what He said to Peter to forgive his enemies. He will truly abide by His own tenets and promises.

"There hath no temptation taken you but such as is common to man: but God is faithful, who will not suffer you to be tempted above that ye are able; but will with the temptation also make a way to escape, that ye may be able to bear it" (1 Corinthians 10:13)

"For sin shall not have dominion over you: for ye are not under the law, but under grace" (Romans 6:14)

"If we say that we have no sin, we deceive ourselves, and the truth is not in us. If we confess our sins, he is faithful and just to forgive us our sins, and to cleanse us from all unrighteousness. If we say that we have not sinned, we make him a liar, and his word is not in us" (1 John 1:8-10)

"Know you not that your bodies are the members of Christ? Shall I then take the members of Christ, and make them the members of a harlot? God forbid". (1 Corinthians 6:15)

None, who is born into this world from a married woman, is without sin; and, therefore, none can become a savior to a sinner. None, who lived a family life, can claim to be a savior of any sinner. No one, except for Lord Jesus Christ, who died on behalf mankind, can be savior to anyone. Many spread good teachings, and ways to avoid suffering, but none, except Lord Jesus Christ, has ever become sacrifice on behalf of man.

Holy Bible deals with the suffering of mankind, suffering of Christ, and salvation from such suffering. Simon Peter, the disciple of Lord Jesus Christ, says that we should arm ourselves with the same kind mind that Lord Jesus Christ had and endured suffering, in order that we may be relieved of sinning. Suffering causes relief from sin.

Lord Jesus, who knew no sin, became sin for us and suffered in order that we may be saved. He not only died, but He was raised from the dead with glorified body, and while He was in the grave His body did not see corruption. It reminds us again that the Lord was born of the Virgin Mary before her union with Joseph to whom she was espoused. He was incarnate God, who died and rose from the dead.

(References: Matthew 16:24; 1 Corinthians 10:13; Romans 6:14; 1 John 1:8-10; 1 Corinthians 6:15)

"Then said Jesus unto his disciples, If any man will come after me, let him deny himself, and take up his cross, and follow me" Matthew 16:24

As for we the believers in Christ, it is to be noted that we are mortals, made of dust, and we will return to dust. However, because we have souls, we will rise up in immortal glorified bodies, when the Lord comes again.

We will rise from the dead, on hearing the loud last trump, when the Lord comes with the sound of an archangel, and if we are alive when the Lord comes will be transformed into glorified bodies and be with the Lord forever, and ever.

We will have immortal bodies, not before our resurrection, but only on resurrection. God promised that we will rise from the dead and will have eternal life in our glorified bodies.

It is wrong teaching that we will become little gods in heaven inasmuch as we are not born into this world as did Jesus of a Virgin mother. We do not die sacrificing our bodies and blood for the sake of others, but suffer in pain for the sins that we have committed. Our suffering is the result of our disobedience of the Lord's commands and statutes. We will be conformed to His image, the image of the Son of God.

The Word of God says that such suffering brings the end of sin in our lives. The Word of God does not tell us that by suffering we would receive salvation, but the Word is telling us that we will cease from sinning due to suffering.

"For whom he did foreknow, he also did predestinate to be conformed to the image of his Son, that he might be the firstborn among many brethren" (Romans 8:29)

SECTION II

SPEAK AS THE ORACLES OF GOD

If any man speak, let him speak as the oracles of God; if any man minister, let him do it as of the ability which God giveth: that God in all things may be glorified through Jesus Christ, to whom be praise and dominion for ever and ever. Amen. (1 Peter 4:11)

CHAPTER 5

SINNER SAVED AND JUSTIFIED

Bible teaches us that a sinner confessing his sins to Lord Jesus and professing that Jesus is Lord and believing in heart that God raised him from the dead is redeemed from the bondage of sin, and justified by God as righteous.

If a man continues to sin he will reap consequences arising out of such sin; nevertheless his salvation is not lost. When a sinner believes in Jesus and His finished works on the cross for his sake, he is dead to sin and alive to Christ. Old man in sinner is crucified, buried and justified as righteous. It is not by good works that a man is saved but by the grace of God through faith in Him.

The law points out sin in us but it does not provide salvation. The law is good, and unless there is law the abrogation of it is not sensed, or felt, or known. In the New Testament it is seen that law is spiritual, and the entire law of Old Testament law is contained in two simple verses.

"Jesus said unto him, Thou shalt love the Lord thy God with all thy heart, and with all thy soul, and with all thy mind. This is the first and great commandment. And the second is like unto it, Thou shalt love thy neighbour as thyself. On these two commandments hang all the law and the prophets" (Matthew 22:37-40)

The Old Testament law has not become lenient in the New Testament as we see in the Sermon on the Mount by Lord Jesus Christ. He said if a man lusts after a woman in his heart it is tantamount to having committed adultery with her already. He said if a man is angry at another man without a cause he is at the risk of facing judgment by God. He said if a man calls another as worthless, or empty headed, he is at the risk of facing court of law, and if a man calls another as fool he is at the risk of being cast into hellfire.

There is a gradual construction seen from Romans Chapter 1 to chapter where it is seen as to how people thinking wise in their own conceit became foolish and sinned greatly. Because they would not get rid of living in sin, God handed them over their lustful desires of the flesh.

It is not that they did not know God; they knew God and in spite of knowing who God is, they did not worship Him; rather they were finding foolishly as to what or how God was like. Because of their reprobate mind their minds became blank and dark. They got confused themselves and claiming to be wise they became great fools. Instead of worshipping God they worshipped idols that were made to look like animals, birds or men or women or even reptiles.

God left them to their own choices to do whatever obnoxious things that their hearts constrained them to do. Their foolishness grew greater than ever before when they did vile things like sharing their bodies with same gender. They traded truth of the knowledge of God to lies. They bowed down to creation rather than to creator.

That is why God gave them over to their own sinful nature and shameful desires of the flesh.

"And likewise also the men, leaving the natural use of the woman, burned in their lust one toward another; men with men working that which is unseemly, and receiving in themselves that recompense of their error which was meet" (Romans 1:27)

People thought to question the existence of God or what or how He looks like. They wanted evidence just as they would see evidences in court of law. Their foolishness to avoid worshipping God resulted in God abandoning them. They were filled with "unrighteousness, fornication, wickedness, covetousness, maliciousness; full of envy, murder, debate, deceit, malignity; whisperers, Backbiters, haters of God, despiteful, proud, boasters, inventors of evil things, disobedient to parents, Without understanding, covenant breakers, without natural affection, implacable, unmerciful" (Romans 1:29-31)

They knew righteous God is not only compassionate and long-suffering but He is consuming fire. They deserve death, and yet they not only commit aforesaid sins, but surprisingly, they take great pleasure in them that commit such sins.

The consequences of sin are very serious; nevertheless, it is for sure that a believer, who is saved will not lose salvation. God will bring him back to His fold either by chastising him physically or mentally or by allowing him to incur serious losses.

Man, then gets frustrated in his life and eventually calls upon God to rescue from the awkward situation he has created for himself, going against the will of God.

That is the same essence Peter was mentioning in 1 Peter Chapter 4 where he dwells on the subject of sin and suffering. He says a man who suffers will cease from sin.

CHAPTER 6

SIN CAN NOT HAVE DOMINION OVER A

CHILD OF GOD

Apostle Paul emphasizes (in Romans 6th chapter) that sin shall not have dominion over born-again child because he/she is not under the law, but under grace. Those who seek to do good works and earn salvation by their own works do nullify the importance of blood of Jesus Christ.

The blood of Jesus Christ that cleanses the sin has no value for them. They diligently keep doing good works in order to receive salvation neglecting the repeated emphasis from the Lord Jesus Christ that there is eternal life only in and through him.

The blood of Jesus shed on the cross of Calvary can only save a person. This is the only way to receive eternal life. Salvation is available to all those who go to him and accept him as the Lord.

Now, here is the question:

After having been delivered from the bondage of sin by grace through faith should a child of God keep sinning because he is under the grace but not under law?

Paul very firmly says, "God forbid". Never should a child of God return to sin and lose blessings from God. Salvation is not lost for those who are saved in the blood of Jesus Christ; however, the Scripture does not endorse repeated sinning. God will surely chide and chastise the one that falls repeatedly into sin and seeks grace time and again.

Should we not consider the fact that if we yield to sin we are servants to sin; and sin becomes our master? We are under grace and we should remain servants to our Lord and be obedient to put on Christ as written in Ephesians 4:24 and live righteous life.

We were, once servants of sin; but after accepting Jesus as our master, we have become servants of righteousness. We should bear fruit unto the Lord by leading a life of holiness and have assurance that there is everlasting life for us in eternity. The law has concluded all of us under sin, but the gift of God is eternal life through Lord Jesus Christ.

We do not know how Far East is from the west but we know that they are opposite poles, and, as born-again children of God, we do know that our sins are removed from us as Far East is from the west. God said that He will never remember our sins after cleansing us from our unrighteousness.

"I, even I, am he that blots out your transgressions for mine own sake, and will not remember thy sins" (Isaiah 43:25)

"For by a single offering he has perfected for all time those who are being sanctified. And the Holy Spirit also bears witness to us; for after saying, "This is the covenant that I will make with them after those days, declares the Lord: I will put my laws on their hearts, and write them on their minds," then he adds, "I will remember their sins and their lawless deeds no more." Hebrews 10:14-17

"Just so, I tell you, there will be more joy in heaven over one sinner who repents than over ninety-nine righteous persons who need no repentance" Luke 15:7

HYPOCRISY IS HATEFUL

"For I say unto you, that except your righteousness shall exceed the righteousness of the scribes and Pharisees, ye shall in no case enter into the kingdom of heaven" (Matthew 5:20)

External depiction of piety, without possessing any character demanded by God, has no value before God. Jesus said Pharisees and Scribes take leadership position such as that of Moses, and demand others to obey Mosaic Law, while they themselves are devoid of observing those laws.

They lay huge burden on others but they themselves do not move a weighty object with any of their fingers. They broaden their phylacteries, and enlarge their borders of their garments, occupy important seats during feasts and in synagogues to be seen of men but lack true devotion to the Lord.

They pay tithe of mint, anise, and cumin to be seen by men, but omit important matters in the Law, judgment, mercy and faith. While they do not feel bad swallowing a camel in their food, they show off as if a fly in their drink is too harmful. This type of attitude is hypocrisy and God hates such an attitude. He needs humble in spirit and kind hearted ones.

Jesus clearly warns that our righteousness should exceed mere hypocrisy and above that was shown by scribes and Pharisees. He said it is they who enter the kingdom of heaven, whether it is in the present age or in the future age.

Circumcision does not make a man Jew, but the character that is built upon God's demands does it. (cf. Matthew 23:1-10, 23, 24; Romans 2:28; Philippians 3:3)

CHAPTER 7

CHASTISEMENT

"My son, despise not the chastening of the LORD; neither be weary of his correction" (Proverbs 3:11)

None of us would like to suffer pain. However, God allows pain in the lives of those who are called according to His purpose. He, being the Father, called us as His "little children", and His dealing with His children is within His authority; it is the family relationship (cf. 1 John 2:1).

The Lord chastens his children, who drift away from His paths, and choose to continue to be in sin. He chastens in order that they may not be lost, but to come back to Him.

Prodigal son wasted his inheritance, and thereafter wished to fill "his belly with the husks that the swine did eat". He realized that there was abundance in his father's house and returned to his father seeking forgiveness, and the father forgave him, and received him gladly. (cf.Luke15:16, 21 and 22). God receives His children when they return to Him in repentance.

In the Old Testament period God's anger burnt on the children of Israel, who worshipped idols, and committed sins; and He chastened them severely.

David was no exception to such chastening when he committed sins. He was forgiven of his sins when he repented; nevertheless he reaped the consequences on this earth. He knew that he was going to be chastened, when he committed sins, and therefore, pleaded for mercy that He may lighten His chastisement.

In Psalm Chapter 6 David prays to God not rebuke him in His anger; neither chasten him in His displeasure. He pleads to God to lighten the severity of His chastisement.

David admitted before the LORD that he was weak, and that his bones were vexed, and his soul was vexed as well. His admittance depicts how much he humbled before the LORD. He questions God as to how long the LORD would keep away from him. He prays very earnestly to the LORD to return to him and deliver his soul. He asks God as to how he would remember the LORD, and give thanks to Him, from his grave, if he died because of chastisement.

David groaned in his spirit, with all the weakness in his body and soul, and says he cried whole night, virtually swimming in the bed soaked with his tears. His eyes became weak, because of his grief and he waxed old, because of all his enemies.

Nonetheless, David becomes self-confident very quickly, and consoles himself saying God heard his weeping and, therefore, commands the evil-doers and workers of iniquity to depart from his presence. He confidently says that the LORD heard his prayer and supplications. Then, he commands his enemies to return their base, and be ashamed, and sore vexed.

Indeed, the LORD does chasten His loved ones when they move away from His presence. He forgives the sins of His children, but He allows scars of the sin to remain in them. God will forget and does not remember our sins; but sinner's own conscience keeps him reminding him of his past sins.

We must seek the Lord's help, when our past sins look upon us with contempt, because God never remembers our sin. It is

Satan, who brings to our memory our past sins in order that we may fall again. The LORD chastens His children in order that they may not commit sins repeatedly.

Apostle Paul comes very heavily on those who repeatedly commit sins even after repenting of their sins with a decision to follow the Lord.

"Moreover the law entered, that the offence might abound. But where sin abounded, grace did much more abound" (Romans 5:20)

"What then? Shall we sin because we are not under the law but under grace? Certainly not!" (Romans 6:15).

CHAPTER 8

LEAD SINLESS LIFE

Leaven symbolizes sin. God's desire was that the children of Israel should be holy, and therefore, it was essential for them to remove entire leaven from their midst before they celebrated the "feast of the unleavened bread". The bread used was without leaven.

The "feast of unleavened bread" is celebrated by the children of Israel for seven days from 15th day of the first month (Abib) to honor the LORD and thank Him for sparing their firstborn from being killed by the LORD on the Passover night. This feast was celebrated with unleavened bread (Exodus 12:15).

The "feast of unleavened bread" was the second feast of the seven feasts listed in Leviticus 23:1-44. The first feast was "Passover", which reminds the children of Israel that their firstborn were saved from death by the LORD when He visited the land of Egypt in His anger to kill the first born of all those, who had not killed the blameless lamb and applied its blood to the lintel posts of their houses.

It was during the tenth plague that God brought upon the land of Egypt that all the firstborn of Egyptians were killed by the LORD because Pharaoh of Egypt continuously refused to deliver them from the bondage of slavery in Egypt. The children of Israel were slaves in Egypt for 400 years, their total sojourn was for 430 years.

God heard their cry and redeemed from the bondage of slavery under Pharaoh. Thus while the firstborn of all the Egyptians, including that of the eldest son of Pharaoh, were killed, all the firstborn of the children of Israel were saved.

The lamb represents Lord Jesus Christ, who was sinless, and without any blemish in Him. He died on behalf of us, in order that we may by accepting Him as Lord and by believing in heart that God raised Him from the dead be saved and receive everlasting life. The Lord became propitiation for us and whoever confessed his sin to the Lord and accepted Him as personal savior is redeemed from the bondage of sin.

Jesus, who was without any blemish was crucified and was buried. His body was in the grave on the 15th day of the first month, and His body in the grave did neither decompose nor corrupted. He was incarnate God and very God Himself. He is He and the Father are one. He was fully divine and fully human (Matthew 27:60)

As for the New Testament believers the bread used in the Lord's Supper does not need to be 'unleavened bread' because those instructions were given to the children of Israel.   The lamb that was sacrificed, was without any blemish, as a type of Jesus.

The New Testament does not teach us to be legalistic in such matters, and obviously where there is no ordinance to do it in a certain way, it does not matter what kind of bread (leavened or unleavened) is used in the Lord's Supper.

There is also another basis not to be legalistic on this matter and it is two different Greek words used for unleavened bread and for ordinary bread. Notice the difference between the usage of the word "bread" in Matthew 26:17 and Matthew 26:26 and in several similar verses.

"Now the first day of the feast of unleavened bread the disciples came to Jesus, saying unto him, Where wilt thou that we prepare for thee to eat the Passover?" (Matthew 26:17)

"And as they were eating, Jesus took bread, and blessed it, and brake it, and gave it to the disciples, and said, Take, eat; this is my body" (Matthew 26:26)

The Greek word used for unleavened bread is "azumos" (Strong's number 106), the Greek word used for the bread that is broken during Lord's Supper is "artos" (Strong's number 740), which is common bread, a loaf.

Romans 14:17-19 says...

"For the kingdom of God is not meat and drink; but righteousness, and peace, and joy in the Holy Ghost. For he, who in these things, serves Christ is acceptable to God, and approved of men. Let us therefore follow after the things which make for peace, and things wherewith one may edify another"

The bread and the cup are the emblems that show the broken body of Lord Jesus Christ and His shed blood on the cross for our redemption. Christ was our Passover Lamb crucified on the cross for our redemption from sin and, therefore, we should live a life of liberation from sin, in joy, praising God that we are redeemed from our sin.

"There is therefore now no condemnation to them which are in Christ Jesus, who walk not after the flesh, but after the Spirit" Romans 8:1.

Scripture exhorts us to examine ourselves and take part in the Lord's Supper worthily in order that we may not eat and drink of it for our damnation. It is imperative that while taking part in the Lord's Supper, one must examine oneself before taking part in the Lord's Supper. This does not preclude born-again children of God from taking part in the Lord's Supper, but it is given as a warning to take part in the Lord's Supper in sincerity and truth. Paul speaks of keeping this feast "not with old leaven, neither of malice and wickedness, but with unleavened bread of sincerity and truth" (cf. 1 Corinthians 5:8)

"But let a man examine himself, and so let him eat of that bread, and drink of that cup. For he that eateth and drinks unworthily, eateth and drinks damnation to himself, not discerning the Lord's body. For this cause many are weak and sickly among you, and many sleep. For if we would judge ourselves, we should not be judged" 1 Corinthians 11:28-31

Paul's main emphasis was that unrepentant sinners in the Church must be put away, after following the guidelines from Matthew Chapter 18, in order that they may not spoil the whole congregation in the Church. Sinner himself is a leaven in the Church, and such notorious sinners, who do not repent of their sins, corrupt all members of the Church with their sinful life and false teachings.

Paul writes in Galatians 5:9 that "A little leaven leavens the whole lump". Leaven is symbolic of sin.

"Purge out therefore the old leaven, that ye may be a new lump, as ye are unleavened. For even Christ our Passover is sacrificed for us: Therefore let us keep the feast, not with old leaven, neither with the leaven of malice and wickedness; but with the unleavened bread of sincerity and truth" 1 Corinthians 5:7-8

CHAPTER 9

DAVID REPENTS

David was a man of wars and God was with him. However, on one occasion when David yielded to Satan's temptation and numbered Israel he had to seek atonement for his sin.

Satan successfully had David yield to his temptation. David in his pride numbered Israel and took boasted of his strength forgetting God. All the days of his life God helped him win the wars with small number in his army.

If we recall David's victory over Goliath, it can be seen that he brought down the proud and hefty Philistine with just one smooth stone out of the five that he has collected from the brook. He put the five stones in a shepherd's bag that he had and swung his sling with just one stone in it and brought down the Philistine onto the ground. Then, David ran and stood upon Goliath and drew the sword from Goliath's sheath and killed him. (1 Samuel 17:40 and 51)

Lord Jesus Christ said, "But when a stronger than he shall come upon him, and overcome him, he taketh from him all his armor wherein he trusted, and divides his spoils". (Luke 11:22)

"And Satan stood up against Israel, and provoked David to number Israel" (1 Chronicles 21:1)

In spite of Joab's efforts to try to prevent David to trespass against God's desires and against Israel, David's orders prevailed and Joab numbered the Israel. God was angry at David and his actions in numbering Israel.

God sent an angel to destroy Jerusalem and as the angel of the LORD was destroying Jerusalem, David repented of the evil he did and said to the angel to stop destroying. He saw the angel of the Lord standing between the earth and heaven having a drawn sword in his hand stretched out over Jerusalem. David and elders of Israel wore sack clothes and fell upon their faces.

David accepted that he sinned against God and prayed that he may be punished but not his people because it was he who sinned against the Lord. The LORD saw that David repented of his sin. (cf. 1 Chronicles 21:26-28)

David was not a perfect man; however, his great sin against Bathsheba and her husband Uriah was forgiven by God when he repented of his sin, He sinned against his flesh and harmed others, but He was all repentant before the LORD. If God could forgive him, then there is no reason why He cannot forgive us of our sins.

<<To the chief Musician, A Psalm of David, when Nathan the prophet came unto him, after he had gone in to Bathsheba.>> "Have mercy upon me, O God, according to thy loving-kindness: according unto the multitude of thy tender mercies blot out my transgressions. Wash me thoroughly from mine iniquity, and cleanse me from my sin. For I acknowledge my transgressions: and my sin is ever before me. Against thee, you only, have I sinned, and done this evil in thy sight: that thou might be justified when thou speaks, and be clear when thou judges. Behold, I was shapen in iniquity; and in sin did my mother conceive me. Behold, thou desires truth in the inward parts: and in the hidden part thou shalt make me to know wisdom. Purge me with hyssop, and I shall be clean: wash me, and I shall be whiter than snow" (Psalms 51:1-7)

He longed to be in the Holy City of Jerusalem; not because it was a royal city but because it was the holy city. His body and soul craved to be in the LORD's dwelling places because they are pleasing and friendly.

There is reconciliation when we pray and accept before God our sins. God forgives us our iniquity.

CHAPTER 10

"A MAN AFTER MINE OWN HEART"

David depended upon God before waging wars. Before he went for war against Philistines he enquired of the Lord saying..,

"Shall I go up to the Philistines?" and God asked him to go ahead.

"And David enquired of the LORD, saying, Shall I go up to the Philistines? Wilt thou deliver them into mine hand? And the LORD said unto David, Go up: for I will doubtless deliver the Philistines into thine hand" (2 Samuel 5:19)

David not only put an end to Philistines who troubled the children of Israel but he also defeated Moabites. He also defeated Hadadezer, the son of Rehob, king of Zobab and recovered his border at the river Euphrates. David smote Syrians and they became servants to David and brought gifts. Edomites also became servants of David and the Almighty God preserved David wherever he went. (Ref. 2 Samuel 8:14)

David dedicated unto God the silver and gold that he had from all nations which he subdued. David's administration and organization was excellent. David administered judgment and justice to all people. (Ref. 2 Samuel 8:11, 15 and 18)

King David's sincere worship of God is seen in many references. He thought of building a temple for God but God allowed his son Solomon to build the temple at Jerusalem.

Speaking to Solomon David said that it was in his mind to build a house unto the name of God, but God said to him that David had shed blood abundantly upon the earth in His sight, and made great wars, and, therefore, he should not build a house unto His name.

God said that his son Solomon would build a house unto the name of the Lord. God promised that He would establish Solomon's throne forever over Israel. He wished that God may give wisdom and understanding to Solomon to keep the law of the Lord. David assured Solomon that if he kept the law of the Lord, he would prosper. He encouraged his son to be of good courage, not to dread, or dismayed. David helped him and said:

"Now, behold, in my trouble I have prepared for the house of the LORD an hundred thousand talents of gold, and a thousand thousand talents of silver; and of brass and iron without weight; for it is in abundance: timber also and stone have I prepared; and you may add thereto" (1 Chronicles 22:14)

God honors who honor him. God blessed David and Solomon abundantly.

"And when he had removed him, he raised up unto them David to be their king; to whom also he gave testimony, and said, I have found David the son of Jesse, a man after mine own heart, which shall fulfil all my will". (Acts 13:22)

CHAPTER 11

A TABLE BEFORE OUR ENEMIES

"You prepare a table before me in the presence of my enemies; you anoint my head with oil; my cup overflows" (Psalm 23:5 ESV)

"My enemies say of me in malice, 'When will he die, and his name perish?' "(Psalm 41:5 ESV)

Do we ever realize that the consequence of our sin frowns upon us and stares in jeer to remind us of our past disobedience of God's commands?

No doubt, God redeems us from hell-fire, when we ask for forgiveness, but the scars of the sin show up on our physical body, if not for our entire life, at least for quite-a-while.

David was so loved by God that the Lord said of him that he was a man after His own heart because He fulfilled His desires of wiping out Amalekites from the face of the earth; but he had to pay heavily for the sins he committed, and in consequence he suffered great agony in his sickbed.

How would God not have mercy on David, who being so a great king over whole of Israel humbled before the LORD and cried saying "...LORD be merciful unto me: heal my soul; for I have sinned against thee"

God is love, merciful, long-suffering and forgave David. He prayed to the LORD to deal with his enemies who ridiculed him saying he was suffering from an evil disease and will never rise from his sickbed.

Even as he was suffering, in his pathetic condition from an unknown sickness, he showers blessings on one, who consider the poor or weak saying the LORD will deliver him in time of trouble.

He was greatly perturbed of his hypocritical friends, who paid called on him, when he was sick. He knew that the LORD will keep him safe and will deliver him from all his enemies. He was critical of his friends, even as they appeared to be honest; nonetheless hypocritical. He was sure that the LORD will make him rise from his sickbed.

"Blessed is the one who considers the poor! In the day of trouble the LORD delivers him; the LORD protects him and keeps him alive; he is called blessed in the land; you do not give him up to the will of his enemies. The LORD sustains him on his sickbed; in his illness you restore him to full health" (Psalm 41:1-3 ESV)

Even when his enemies spoke of him in derision as to who would help him rise form his bed in his sickness, and when his dearest friend whom he trusted had lifted up his heel against him, he prays to the LORD to be merciful to him and raise him up from the bed in order that he may repay them in their own coin.

This was a prophecy uttered by David about Judas Iscariot, who in future, being a disciple of Jesus, would betray the Lord. Quoting this verse John writes that the prophecy was fulfilled.

"Yea, mine own familiar friend, in whom I trusted, which did eat of my bread, hath lifted up his heel against me". (Psalms 41:9)

"I speak not of you all: I know whom I have chosen: but that the scripture may be fulfilled, He that eateth bread with me hath lifted up his heel against me" (John 13:18)

David knew that God will favor him and support Him with His mighty hand and in recognition he says with confidence that his enemy will not be triumphant over him.

He has confidence that God will uphold him in his integrity, and sets him before His face forever. He had earlier said...

"Surely goodness and mercy shall follow me all the days of my life: and I will dwell in the house of the LORD forever" (Psalms 23:6)

 He now worships the LORD by saying...

"Blessed be the LORD God of Israel from everlasting, and to everlasting. Amen, and Amen" Psalm 41:13

Priest Zacharias prophesied about the Son of God Lord Jesus Christ that He is the redeemer. In fulfillment of many prophesies Lord Jesus, who relinquished His glory with the Father, came down to this earth in the form of servant, and in the likeness of man, to save mankind by becoming by becoming a substitute to bear their sins and die on behalf of them.

Jesus was crucified, was buried and was raised by God on the third day.

"Blessed be the Lord God of Israel; for he hath visited and redeemed his people, And hath raised up an horn of salvation for us in the house of his servant David" (Luke 1:68-69)

Apostle Paul writes that whoever acknowledges by mouth that Jesus is the Lord, and believe in heart that God raised Him from the dead on the third day will be saved. (cf. Romans 10:9)

Psalmist prophesied and said...

"He also exalts the horn of his people, the praise of all his saints; even of the children of Israel, a people near unto him. Praise you the LORD" (Psalms 148:14)

CHAPTER 12

DOES GOD ANSWER ALL OUR PRAYERS

As the widow at Zarephath and her son continued to live happily with the blessings from the LORD through Elijah the prophet, there came the days of sorrow, when her son fell severely ill and died.

The widow was sore depressed and vexed with him. She questioned him as to what wrong she had done to him that he came to their home, and if that was to bring to her remembrance her sin, which may have caused death of her son. Perturbed by the question from the widow, Elijah said to her to give her son to him, and when she gave the child into his arms, he took the child to the room where he stayed. He laid her son on his bed and cried to the LORD saying "O LORD my God, have you brought calamity even upon the widow with whom I sojourn, by killing her son?"

After submitting his supplication to the LORD Elijah stretched himself upon the child three times and cried to the LORD, "O LORD my God, let this child's life come into him again." The LORD answered his prayer and the child's life came back and he lived.

Elijah brought the live child to the woman downstairs and gave him to her and said "See, your son lives." The dead son of the widow was raised to life, and when the woman saw her son live she was exceedingly happy. In her remorse she said to Elijah that she, then, believed that he was a man of God, and the Truth, which was the word of the LORD, was in his mouth (cf. 1 Kings 17:17-24 ESV)

Elijah's prayer teaches us that God grants answers to our prayer provided it is according to His will. He gives us that which we ask if it is in His will. "And this is the confidence that we have in him, that, if we ask any thing according to his will, he heareth us" (1 John 5:14)

Much controversy is heard in our circles from a passage from James (James 5:13-20), which refers Elijah's prayer. It poses serious questions as to whether sick will be healed when he is prayed over. James who was half-brother and servant of Lord Jesus Christ writes that if we pray to the Lord in faith He will grant our prayers. Controversy is seen because most of the times we read such passages without understanding what they are really saying.

There are few points that need our attention.

Firstly, it is an admonition for the sick himself to pray over his sickness. It is personal relationship of an individual with God that matters more than someone else or elders praying for the individual. God and the individual only know clearly whether the individual does or does not have right relationship with God.

Secondly, the sick has to call for the elders of the church and let them pray over him. Notice, here it is the not the elders of the church who need to take initiative to pray over him; but it is the individual suffering who is sick should "call for the elders of the church, and let them pray over him". The text needs to be read as it is presented to us; and not the way we want it to say.

Elders or church members might visit the sick as a courtesy or love and affection toward the sick, but the onus of calling the elders or the church members to pray over him or request for prayers rests with the individual. Additionally, even as the manners of this world demand, no one would like to gate-crash into the house of the one who is sick, but would like to visit the sick at his/her invitation.

Thirdly, it is by anointing him with oil in the name of the Lord. What does anointing with oil mean here? The word "anointing" is a translation of the Greek word Strong's# 218 "aleipho". The word here does not mean consecration of an individual or vessels for holy purpose as was done in the Old Testament period, or anointing kings such as the one performed on Saul or David, or as Lord Jesus Christ quotes a prophesy about His anointing as we read in Luke 4:16-20.

"The Spirit of the Lord is upon me, because he hath anointed me to preach the gospel to the poor; he hath sent me to heal the brokenhearted, to preach deliverance to the captives, and recovering of sight to the blind, to set at liberty them that are bruised" (Luke 4:18)

The anointing that James referred was like applying oil for medicinal purposes. Olive oil was used for medicinal purposes and the intention was using this word here was in the sense of applying oil to look fresh and have the medicinal effects of the oil or in reverence to the Lord (cf. Mar 6:13; Lu 4:18; 7:38,46; Joh 1:41; 9:6,11; 11:2; 12:3; Ac 4:27; 10:38; 2Co 1:21; Heb. 1:9)

"When he had thus spoken, he spat on the ground, and made clay of the spittle, and he anointed the eyes of the blind man with the clay" (John 9:6)

Fourthly, it is clearly addressed to the individual that his/her prayer in faith will save him/her and the Lord will raise him up. The phrase used here is "the prayer of the faith will save the one who is sick". Fifthly, if the individual who is sick has committed sins he will be forgiven when he prays for himself.

Sixthly, "confess your sins" or "faults to one another", does not mean an individual has to confess his sins to any pastor, priest or to any individual. It only means if we have offended someone we have to seek forgiveness from him of that particular offence that we caused to him. Secret sins should be confessed only to God through Lord Jesus Christ. We have only one mediator for us; and He is our Lord Jesus Christ, who justifies us before the Father.

Jesus said: "But I say to you that everyone who is angry with his brother will be liable to judgment; whoever insults his brother will be liable to the council; and whoever says, 'You fool!' will be liable to the hell of fire. So if you are offering your gift at the altar and there remember that your brother has something against you, leave your gift there before the altar and go. First be reconciled to your brother, and then come and offer your gift" (Matthew 5:22-24 ESV)

Citing as to why many are weak or sick among us or die, Paul warns us to examine ourselves before we eat of the bread and drink of the cup during Lord's Supper.

"Whoever, therefore, eats the bread or drinks the cup of the Lord in an unworthy manner will be guilty concerning the body and blood of the Lord. Let a person examine himself, then, and so eat of the bread and drink of the cup. For anyone who eats and drinks without discerning the body eats and drinks judgment on himself" (1 Corinthians 11:27-29 ESV)

It is imperative that we obey the commandments of Lord Jesus Christ and instructions of Apostle Paul in order to be healed of our sickness. "Therefore, confess your sins to one another and pray for one another, that you may be healed".

The prayer of the righteous person and his fervent supplication has great power and it surely works in the way God wants it to work. Not every prayer is answered according to the wish of the person praying and this secret is known only to the Almighty God; but surely it is worth noting that everything works for good for those who believe in Him.

"And we know that to them that love God all things work together for good, even to them that are called according to his purpose" (Romans 8:28)

Paul's prayer was not answered in the way he wanted it to be, but was answered the way the Lord wanted. Paul prayed three times to remove the thorn in his flesh, but the Lord said in his weakness the Lord's name was glorified.

"And by reason of the exceeding greatness of the revelations, that I should not be exalted overmuch, there was given to me a thorn in the flesh, a messenger of Satan to buffet me, that I should not be exalted overmuch. Concerning this thing I besought the Lord thrice, that it might depart from me. And he hath said unto me, My grace is sufficient for thee: for my power is made perfect in weakness. Most gladly therefore will I rather glory in my weaknesses, that the power of Christ may rest upon me. Wherefore I take pleasure in weaknesses, in injuries, in necessities, in persecutions, in distresses, for Christ's sake: for when I am weak, then am I strong" (2 Corinthians 12:7-10)

The mother of James and Zebedee asked Lord Jesus to seat them one on the right hand side of the Lord and other on the left hand side of the Lord in eternity; but her prayer was denied by the Lord. (cf. Matthew 20:20-24)

James quotes prayer of Elijah, who was a man like us and yet prayed fervently that it might not rain for three and half years and his prayer was answered by God. It did not rain for three and half years; and when he prayed again that it might rain God answered his prayer and it rained and the earth bore fruit.

"Elijah was a man with a nature like ours, and he prayed fervently that it might not rain, and for three years and six months it did not rain on the earth. Then he prayed again, and heaven gave rain, and the earth bore its fruit" (James 5:17-18 ESV)

CHATER 13

MAIMING ORGANS?

"And if thy right eye offend thee, pluck it out, and cast it from thee: for it is profitable for thee that one of thy members should perish, and not that thy whole body should be cast into hell. And if thy right hand offend thee, cut it off, and cast it from thee: for it is profitable for thee that one of thy members should perish, and not that thy whole body should be cast into hell". (Matthew 5:29-30)

The essence of the above two verses should be understood clearly as to what the intention of God is, rather than interpreting literally to maim the organs. Jesus was a Jew and He was addressing Jewish disciples, and therefore, the context and the premise should be kept in mind while interpreting the instructions in these verses. Jews, very often, represented their emotions with the members of the body. The right eye and the right hand form very essential members of the body.

Comparing with other references, such as Romans 6:13; 7:23; 2Pe 2:14 would help us understand how to interpret such complex issues. In Jewish tradition, bowels represented compassion; the heart represented understanding, feeling, secret purpose and affection; the eye denotes envy (cf. Matt.20:15), evil passion, or sin (cf. Mark 7:21-22)

Lord Jesus was telling us here that in case where these organs offend (displease us or cause us to sin, such as lusting after a woman with eyes) then, we better abandon them and overcome passions arising out of such lustful fleshly desires rather than pursuing them.

"Mortify therefore your members which are upon the earth; fornication, uncleanness, inordinate affection, evil concupiscence, and covetousness, which is idolatry" (Colossians 3:5)

Sin causes greater damage to man than to have the said organs to intentionally commit sin. That is why the Lord says it is better to pluck out right eye and go to heaven rather than possessing it and lust after a woman ending up life after death in hell to suffer eternally. Likewise if right causes to commit sin, better cut it off and reach heaven rather than ending up in hell with both the hands.

The very fact that a man's physical body dissolves fully and he does not rise (whether in the case of born-again believer or in the case of unsaved man) indicates that literal interpretation is not meant here.

The mortal bodies that we have will be dissolved after death, and everyone will rise or be transformed to immortal bodies. In the case of believers they receive immortal glorified bodies, and in the case of unbelievers they rise in spirit and in a body not known to any human being, and face condemnation, and eventually everlasting gnashing of teeth and suffer in fire that never gets quenched.

Therefore, the essence of Matthew 5:29-30 is that even if we were to cut off our inevitable body parts we should never choose to sin and suffer eternally.

Lord Jesus Christ was sinless and He, being in the likeness of man took upon Himself our sin, and died for our sake. Anyone who confesses Jesus as Lord and believes in heart that God raised Him from the dead will receive salvation. Christ suffered for our sake, and was buried. He was raised not in fleshly body but in glorified body.

When the Lord was on the cross, he was suffering just as a man would, because our sin was upon Him.

"For he hath made him to be sin for us, who knew no sin; that we might be made the righteousness of God in him" (2 Corinthians 5:21)

That is the reason why refused to drink the stupefying drink given to Him, in order to alleviate pain. His legs were not broken to fulfill the prophecy. He was not hung at the end of the Passover day, but was removed as dead body from the cross at the commencement of the feast of the leaven began. He was in the grave for three days, and three nights, just as Jonah was in the belly for three days.

"For as Jonas was three days and three nights in the whale's belly; so shall the Son of man be three days and three nights in the heart of the earth" (Matthew 12:40)

The three days and three nights are not according to man's calendar, but according to Jewish calendar wherein day or night or part of the day or part of the night were counted as day or night respectively.

The Spirit of the Lord went to lower parts of the earth, and preached His victory message to the spirits in prison. His body did not get corrupted in the grave, and God raised Him from the dead on the third day. Esther 4:16, 5:1 would give some insight into what it means three days and three nights.

"Go, gather together all the Jews that are present in Shushan, and fast ye for me, and neither eat nor drink three days, night or day: I also and my maidens will fast likewise; and so will I go in unto the king, which is not according to the law: and if I perish, I perish" (Esther 4:16)

"Now it came to pass on the third day, that Esther put on her royal apparel, and stood in the inner court of the king's house, over against the king's house: and the king sat upon his royal throne in the royal house, over against the gate of the house" (Esther 5:1)

CHAPTER 14

NO ONE CAN SERVE TWO MASTERS

"Lay not up for yourselves treasures upon earth, where moth and rust doth corrupt, and where thieves break through and steal: But lay up for yourselves treasures in heaven, where neither moth nor rust doth corrupt, and where thieves do not break through nor steal: For where your treasure is, there will your heart be also. The light of the body is the eye: if therefore thine eye be single, thy whole body shall be full of light. But if thine eye be evil, thy whole body shall be full of darkness. If therefore the light that is in thee be darkness, how great is that darkness! No man can serve two masters: for either he will hate the one, and love the other; or else he will hold to the one, and despise the other. Ye cannot serve God and mammon" (Matthew 6:19-24)

"No man can serve two masters: for either he will hate the one, and love the other; or else he will hold to the one, and despise the other. Ye cannot serve God and mammon" (Matthew 6:24)

God loved Israel and said to them that if they obey Him and keep His statutes He will bless them; otherwise, He will turn against them.

To the very God who blessed them they rendered shame, mockery and insult. They built altars to idols and worshipped them instead of offering sacrifices and oblation to the living God and, therefore, God took away from them their altars and temples.

The division of the kingdom of Israel began with King Solomon performing abominable acts before the LORD. It was because Solomon's loathsome actions that led to the destruction of the unified Kingdom of Israel gradually ending in the Solomon's Temple becoming a by-gone word, and the kingdom dividing into two.

God raised Jeroboam, who was Solomon's trusted aide appointed as supervisor over the laborers from the house of Joseph, as the greatest adversaries of him (Ref. 1 Kings 11:28)

"But it shall come to pass, if thou wilt not hearken unto the voice of the LORD thy God, to observe to do all his commandments and his statutes which I command thee this day; that all these curses shall come upon thee, and overtake thee" (Deuteronomy 28:15)

After the death of Solomon his son Rehoboam offended Jeroboam by levying taxes on the ten tribes of Israel more than his father did. The Ten tribes of Israel led by Jeroboam rebelled against Rehoboam and formed the Northern Kingdom.

The rebellion resulted in the Southern Kingdom with only two tribes i.e. Judah and Benjamin in the Southern Kingdom. Jeroboam became the king over the "House of Israel" which was Northern kingdom while Rehoboam was the king of "House of Judah". The Levites mixed up on both the sides.

None of the kings of Israel from Jeroboam to the last king Hoshea did what was right in the sight of the LORD and eventually the Northern Kingdom (House of Israel) was taken over by Assyrians and God scattered the "House of Israel". God addressed the disobedience and idolatry of the "House of Israel" most of the time calling it as "Ephraim".

Israel did not bring any fruit for others but only for themselves. Judah followed Israel in disobeying the Lord. God grieved over the retardation of the commitment of both Israel and Judah and handed them over as captives to Assyrians and Babylonians respectively. Later Babylonians subdued Assyrians and Nineveh, capital city of Assyria was destroyed beyond recognition.

There were giants and mighty men in Canaan, and God gave Israel the Promised Land, Canaan, flowing with milk and honey and goodly things but with the very goodly things received from God they made goodly images of idols and worshipped them.

Israel's heart was divided with their devotion partly towards God and partly to idols. Bible says no man can serve two masters. Jesus said no man can serve both God and money. Either man will serve God or Satan.

"Now therefore, if ye will obey my voice indeed, and keep my covenant, then ye shall be a peculiar treasure unto me above all people: for all the earth is mine" (Exodus 19:5)

CHAPTER 15

ARE MIRACLES CEASED?

Miracles have not ceased. My personal testimony is that God helped me and blessed me wonderfully in my life in several areas. I desire to share here about healing by miracles.

I am a living miracle of God's grace in healing. More than twenty years ago I had kidney transplant — not the greatness of medical science! It is all by the grace of God! God works in different ways in different individuals. If it was greatness of medical science all the cases of kidney transplant should have been successful to live as many years as I lived until now.

There is a great deal of misunderstanding that miracles ceased and healing ceased. It is because faith-healers try to command God in the name of Jesus to heal the sick. God will hear our prayers, but one cannot treat God as a slave to obey man's command and heal the sick!

There are great number of faith-healers, false pretenders, and charlatans, (as many quacks as in medical field) who manipulate events to lead in believing that it is by faith-healers command that sick are healed. They deceive men that there is instant healing of all the diseases, and that by their command, God obeys them and heals them. It should be noted that God answers prayers according to His purposes, and never according to the commands of men to God.

My kidney donor was not my relative. Believe it or not, that donor came to me and said God sent him to me, and he will give one of his kidneys to me and then only he will go. He did exactly as he promised.

"For my thoughts are not your thoughts, neither are your ways my ways, saith the LORD" (Isaiah 55:8))

I still wonder who that donor was! I am sure he was led by the Spirit of God to give one of his kidneys to me. We pursued the case with Tamil Nadu Government in India and after successfully passing their regulations and conditions laid down for us to pass, I had kidney transplant done in 1997 after 84 dialyses.

WHAT ABOUT PHYSICAL HEALING?

Do or do not Isaiah 53:4, 5 and 1 Peter 2:24 refer to physical healing?

"Surely he hath borne our griefs, and carried our sorrows: yet we did esteem him stricken, smitten of God, and afflicted" (Isaiah 53:4)

"But he was wounded for our transgressions, he was bruised for our iniquities: the chastisement of our peace was upon him; and with his stripes we are healed" (Isaiah 53:5)

"Who his own self bare our sins in his own body on the tree that we, being dead to sins, should live unto righteousness: by whose stripes ye were healed" (1 Peter 2:24)

By His stripes we are healed from our sin and it is the spiritual healing. The Lord by washing our sins, restored us to the favor of The Father. The healing, in terms of the Bible verses, is frequently represented an act of healing from sin, which in itself is a disease. David says...

"Have mercy upon me, O LORD; for I am weak: O LORD, heal me; for my bones are vexed. (Psalms 6:2)

"I said, LORD, be merciful unto me: heal my soul; for I have sinned against thee" (Psalms 41:4)

"Who forgives all thine iniquities; who heals all thy diseases" (Psalms 103:3)

Essentially, the meaning of the above verses is that Messiah was to be scourged on behalf of us as per prophecies, and the prophecies were fulfilled. By His sufferings, our sin is healed and we are blessed with spiritual health. In our resurrection we will have glorified bodies and will have everlasting life. It is in eternity that we will have no pain, no suffering and no death.

Sickness cannot be avoided by believers. Scriptures say all of us have sinned, we who have body made of out dust, will suffer in our bodies. Isiah 53:5 and 1 Peter 2:24 are referring to the promise God made that our salvation is secure and we will have perfect sanctification in eternity. We have the promise that we will see Lord Jesus Christ, when He comes again, face to face and will be confirmed to His image. We are saved by grace through faith.

"Being confident of this very thing, that he which hath begun a good work in you will perform it until the day of Jesus Christ" (Philippians 1:6)

"In whom ye also trusted, after that ye heard the word of truth, the gospel of your salvation: in whom also after that ye believed, ye were sealed with that holy Spirit of promise, Which is the earnest of our inheritance until the redemption of the purchased possession, unto the praise of his glory" (Ephesians 1:13-14)

"For whom he did foreknow, he also did predestinate to be conformed to the image of his Son, that he might be the firstborn among many brethren" (Romans 8:29)

Those who are saved by the grace of God are healed of their sin. Paul advises Timothy, whom he considered as his son in faith, to have little wine for his stomach's sake. Trophimus, who was a seven-year companion of Paul, was sick and Paul says he should be left in Mellitus.

"Drink no longer water, but use a little wine for thy stomach's sake and thine often infirmities" (1 Timothy 5:23)

"Erastus abode at Corinth: but Trophimus have I left at Miletus sick" (2 Timothy 4:20)

"Let the wicked forsake his way, and the unrighteous man his thoughts: and let him return unto the LORD, and he will have mercy upon him; and to our God, for he will abundantly pardon" (Isaiah 55:7)

Paul had a "thorn" in his flesh and when he prayed to God, the Lord said to him "my grace is sufficient for you" rather than removing the "thorn" from his flesh. Paul never complained again, he continued to reap the blessings from God. Truly, God's grace was sufficient for him.

"And lest I should be exalted above measure through the abundance of the revelations, there was given to me a thorn in the flesh, the messenger of Satan to buffet me, lest I should be exalted above measure. For this thing I besought the Lord thrice, that it might depart from me. And he said unto me, My grace is sufficient for thee: for my strength is made perfect in weakness. Most gladly therefore will I rather glory in my infirmities, that the power of Christ may rest upon me" (2 Corinthians 12:7-9)

There is no reason why someone should doubt God's willingness to pardon abundantly. Even though wicked man's ways seem to be unpardonable, yet God in His mercy forgives a repentant sinner. Lord Jesus took upon Himself our sin even though He was sinless and knew no sin in order that we may be made the righteousness of God in Him. David prayed to God to forgive his sin, which was indeed great! We are justified by His blood and will be saved from wrath through Him.

"For he hath made him to be sin for us, who knew no sin; that we might be made the righteousness of God in him" (2 Corinthians 5:21)

"For thy name's sake, O LORD, pardon mine iniquity; for it is great" (Psalms 25:11)

Much more then, being now justified by his blood, we shall be saved from wrath through him. (Romans 5:9)

CHAPTER 16

PROPHECY FULFILLED

"That it might be fulfilled which was spoken by Esaias the prophet, saying, Himself took our infirmities, and bare our sicknesses" (Matthew 8:17)

Matthew 8:17 is fulfillment of Prophecy in Isaiah 53:4 and 5

"Surely he hath borne our griefs, and carried our sorrows: yet we did esteem him stricken, smitten of God, and afflicted. But he was wounded for our transgressions, he was bruised for our iniquities: the chastisement of our peace was upon him; and with his stripes we are healed" (Isaiah 53:4-5)

Prophet Isaiah lays out clearly the doctrine of atonement. He prophesied that Messiah was to bear our griefs, sorrows and our sin. This also corroborates with the 2 Corinthians 5:21

"For he hath made him to be sin for us, who knew no sin; that we might be made the righteousness of God in him" (2 Corinthians 5:21)

Matthew 8:17 is taken out of context and grossly misinterpreted by some Christians that Lord Jesus healed everyone by his death on the cross and His healing was voluntary, nay, that is not right! Surely Lord Jesus took our infirmities and bore our sickness, but was it for everyone in the world? Pondering over the context in which it is written shows that only those who were brought to Him, and only on whom He had compassion, were healed by Him.

The griefs and infirmities are the diseases of the body. Therefore, it can be conclusively said that by Jesus becoming sin for us, we are made righteous, and our sickness was borne by Him, which is to say that our sin was removed, upon our confession that Jesus is Lord and God raised Him from the dead on the third day. The cause of all sorrows and griefs of those that needed healing was because of their sin. When Lord Jesus paid for our sin, it is also tantamount to paying not only for the redemption of our soul, but for our bodies as well. Our bodies will be transformed to glorified bodies only at our resurrection.

It is worth reading and understanding John 1:29; and 1 Peter 2:24

The next day John sees Jesus coming unto him, and saith, Behold the Lamb of God, which taketh away the sin of the world. (John 1:29)

"Who his own self bare our sins in his own body on the tree that we, being dead to sins, should live unto righteousness: by whose stripes ye were healed" (1 Peter 2:24)

PASSAGE 1

The context in which Matthew 8:17 appears is as follows:

"And when Jesus was come into Peter's house, he saw his wife's mother laid, and sick of a fever. And he touched her hand, and the fever left her: and she arose, and ministered unto them. When the even was come, they brought unto him many that were possessed with devils: and he cast out the spirits with his word, and healed all that were sick: That it might be fulfilled which was spoken by Esaias the prophet, saying, Himself took our infirmities, and bare our sicknesses" (Matthew 8:14-17)

First of all, it was Peter's house. Jesus went into the house of Peter. He saw Peter's mother-in-law was laid with fever. (It clearly suggests that disciples of Jesus Christ can marry and own houses). Jesus had compassion on Peter's mother-in-law and touched her hand and fever left her. The text that follows is that she arose and ministered unto them and at evening, many, who were possessed with devils, were brought to him, and the Lord cast out the spirits with His word and healed all that were sick. Note again, it was in the house of Peter. People brought who needed healing to the Lord. The Lord healed all those who were brought to Him.

PASSAGE 2

Lord Jesus healed only few

"And he went out from thence, and came into his own country; and his disciples follow him. And when the Sabbath day was come, he began to teach in the synagogue: and many hearing him were astonished, saying, from whence hath this man these things? And what wisdom is this which is given unto him, that even such mighty works are wrought by his hands? Is not this the carpenter, the son of Mary, the brother of James, and Joses, and of Juda, and Simon? and are not his sisters here with us? And they were offended at him. But Jesus said unto them, a prophet is not without honor, but in his own country, and among his own kin, and in his own house. And he could there do no mighty work, save that he laid his hands upon a few sick folk, and healed them. And he marveled because of their unbelief. And he went round about the villages, teaching" (Mark 6:1-6)

Notice that the healing referred to in this passage are done in the home town of Lord Jesus Christ. He could have done "mighty" works there, but He did not. The Lord "laid hands upon a few sick folk and healed them". There are multiple accounts of His healing sick, but the Lord healed only those who were brought to Him. It shows clearly that to receive healing the sick must to Him, or be brought to Him first. Lord Jesus Christ's showing of compassion follows then, and heals them. Based on Mark 6:1-6 it could also be deduced that He does not heal everyone. Just because the Lord entered His hometown does not mean that everyone who needed healing in his home town were healed. There was a role to be played by the one who needed healing; and it was to go to Him and obey Him or pray to Him to heal. "And he could there do no mighty work, save that he laid his hands upon a few sick folk, and healed them"

PASSAGE 3

Draw Near to God and he will draw near to you.

"But he giveth more grace. Wherefore he saith, God resists the proud, but giveth grace unto the humble. Submit yourselves therefore to God. Resist the devil, and he will flee from you. Draw nigh to God, and he will draw nigh to you. Cleanse your hands, ye sinners; and purify your hearts, ye double minded. Be afflicted, and mourn, and weep: let your laughter be turned to mourning, and your joy to heaviness. Humble yourselves in the sight of the Lord, and he shall lift you up" (James 4:6-10)

"Is any sick among you? Let him call for the elders of the church; and let them pray over him, anointing him with oil in the name of the Lord" (James 5:14)

CHAPTER 17

CORRECT THINKING

It is imperative that we consider the life of Lord Jesus Christ, who armed Himself with Spiritual warfare and suffered on this earth. His life was victorious. There was a goal set for Him, and it was a joyous life, authoritative life in heaven. After His suffering and crucifixion, the Lord ascended into heaven and is seated on the right hand of God. He is given authority to all powers and angels.

One important fact we should remember is that our souls are redeemed from perishing when we are born-again; however, the body is not redeemed from its sinful nature. We will have our glorified bodies when we resurrect from the dead when Jesus comes again, or those who are alive at the time of His coming are 'caught up' to be with Him forever and ever.

Therefore, physical suffering on this earth is inevitable. It is in this context that the Bible says we should be armed with spiritual warfare to encounter the temptations of Satan.

Lord Jesus Christ armed Himself not because He was a sinner, but He was made sin for us. He suffered on behalf of us on the cross that we, who have confessed Jesus as Lord and believed in heart that God raised Him from the dead on the third day, will receive everlasting life to be with Him and reign with Him. We will be kings and priests in His kingdom. It is that hope we have in Him.

Suffering loosens from the grip of sin. Suffering prevents us to live in sin and, therefore, we no longer live in sin. Suffering makes a believer to get out of the vulnerability to commit sin. The creator of this world, took upon Himself our sin and suffered on behalf us, and therefore, we have salvation.

Christ's suffering redeemed our souls from sin. It does not mean our mortal bodies have become immortal immediately after becoming the children of God. We have to live out the life given to us by the Lord in the sinful world, and therefore, we need His grace every day.

Our bodies are made of dust, and not until our physical death, and until Lord Jesus Christ descends "from heaven with a shout, with the voice of the archangel, and with the trump of God" when the dead in Christ shall rise, and those, who are alive at that point of time, "shall be caught up together with them in the clouds, to meet the Lord in the air: and so shall we ever be with the Lord" we will have mortal bodies, and immediately after that we will live in transformed and glorified bodies, which will not suffer any pain or death (cf. 1 Thessalonians 4:16-17; Revelation 21:4)

"And God shall wipe away all tears from their eyes; and there shall be no more death, neither sorrow, nor crying, neither shall there be any more pain: for the former things are passed away" (Revelation 21:4)

Lord Jesus Christ saw value in suffering, He saw that a joy was set before Him.

"For it became him, for whom are all things, and by whom are all things, in bringing many sons unto glory, to make the captain of their salvation perfect through sufferings" (Hebrews 2:10)

"Looking unto Jesus the author and finisher of our faith; who for the joy that was set before him endured the cross, despising the shame, and is set down at the right hand of the throne of God" (Hebrews 12:2)

CHAPTER 18

SAVED BY GRACE

"And certain men which came down from Judaea taught the brethren, and said, except ye be circumcised after the manner of Moses, ye cannot be saved". (Acts 15:1)

"O foolish Galatians, who hath bewitched you, that ye should not obey the truth, before whose eyes Jesus Christ hath been evidently set forth, crucified among you?" (Galatians 3:1)

Apostle Paul admonishes Galatians in no uncertain terms for believing in works associated with salvation. The word he used is 'bewitched'. He was not only asking them as to who has cast a spell over their understanding or enchantment, or fascinated them about their belief that law would save them and works were associated with their salvation, but called them 'fools' (Galatians 3:1) for such belief as they hold that law and works could save them.

(The word 'fools' used here does not demean them that they lack wisdom and prudence, but he demeans their misunderstanding that they must do something under the law to God in recompense to what he has done for us. The meaning of 'fool' here was similar to what Jesus meant in Matthew 7:26.)

"And everyone who hears these words of mine and does not do them will be like a foolish man who built his house on the sand" (Matthew 7:26 ESV)

The whole chapter of Galatians 3 deals with this subject of law versus grace. Paul not only questions them if there is anyone in the world, who is perfect in flesh, but also provides answers to his questions that no one could be saved by the law and works associated with it. He goes on to say that only faith in Jesus Christ, who redeemed us from the curse of the law, could save us.

Abraham believed God, and it was reckoned unto him as righteousness. He says that the children, who are of faith, are the children of Abraham.

The Scriptures foresaw that God would justify the heathen through faith, and made available to us, the Word, through preaching, and made available this preaching even before the proclamation of the gospel unto Abraham that in him shall all nations be blessed. Obviously, this indicates that those, who are of faith in Christ, are blessed with the kind of faith Abraham had.

inasmuch as it written in the Scriptures that whosoever continues to believe that one would become perfect by being obedient to the commands written in the Law, is cursed, because, in spite of Christ has redeemed us from the bondage of the Law, he is still subjecting himself to be under the curse.

Law points to the sin but it cannot save anyone; it is only grace through faith that we receive salvation because no one, who desires to be judged under the law, can be justified as righteous before God. The just shall live by faith and it is certain that the law is not of faith, but whosoever, tries to believe that law would save him would live by the law and would be under the curse.

Lord Jesus indeed came to save his own, but when they rejected him, salvation was made available for Gentiles. No doubt this was in the plan of God, and this mystery was revealed in Romans 11:6-11. He came into this world to provide a way out from these stringent laws, and provided a way for everyone, that by faith in him a person is saved by grace.

Lord Jesus was hung on the cross and bore our sins so that we may not be under the curse. It is written that 'cursed is everyone that hangs on a tree'. He came into this world so that the blessing of Abraham would be available for Gentiles through him, and that the gentiles may also receive the promise of the Spirit through faith.

CHAPTER 19

LAW WAS OUR SCHOOLMASTER

"Wherefore the law was our schoolmaster to bring us unto Christ, that we might be justified by faith". (Galatians 3:24)

A frequently asked question is that why God gave law in the first place, and then the Bible later claims that we are saved by grace through faith.

Apostle Paul clarifies this dilemma in the Book of Galatians that the law is not against the promises of God, but it was given that man may understand that the transgressions he committed cannot be forgiven by law, which only points out the guilt of a person. Law does not provide salvation.

Man can never be saved from his past transgressions of God's commands by keeping the law and he will never be able to keep the law to its perfection.

Under the law priest had to offer sacrifice first for himself, and then offer a sacrifice for the person, who is guilty of committing transgression of the law.

If law were sufficient to make a man righteous, then righteousness should have been by keeping the law, but inasmuch as no one can keep the law to its perfection, none can be counted as righteous except by the grace of God.

The scriptures, therefore, have concluded as all have committed transgression of God's commands. The inference is that all are sinners unless saved from the wrath of God, who alone can forgive transgression of His commandments.

The promise by faith of Lord Jesus Christ was made available only to those who believe in Him. The law was like our schoolmaster who teaches us the way unto Jesus Christ. The incarnate God, Lord Jesus Christ, who came into this world in the likeness of man, and offered Himself as a sacrifice on behalf of all, who have sinned, is the only mediator between God and man.

However, His death on the cross has not automatically made everyone righteous. His righteousness is imputed to the sinner, only when he repents of his sin, and confesses by mouth that Jesus is Lord, and God raised Him from the dead on the third day (cf. Romans 10:9-10).

The lamb offered as sacrifice in the Old Testament period was a type of substitutionary offering of sacrifice on behalf of sinner. There is no salvation unless blood was shed of the lamb, and even so, the sacrifices were repeatedly offered by individuals, and once every year by the high priest, the sin of individual, or the nation, was only covered and was not removed fully.

The complete removal of the sin from a sinner can be only when a man believes in the perfect sacrifice of Lord Jesus Christ, the Son of God, who became sin for us, and our sin was judged on the cross.

We can be justified only by faith in him. After Jesus had become propitiation for us, it is not required of us to do what is to be done under the law in order to have salvation; but faith in him alone is enough and that is to say that we are no longer under schoolmaster.

As many as have confessed that Jesus Christ is the Lord, and believed that God raised Him from the dead are saved, irrespective of whether or not one who believed in Him is a Jew or Gentile, bonded or free, male or female.

All those, who are saved by the precious blood of Jesus Christ are called "One New Man" in Him. They all belong to Him. We, who have become one such "New Man" in Him are called Abraham's seed by faith and have inherited God's promises. Apostle Paul blesses all those, who accept Lord Jesus Christ's death on the cross, as the basis for their salvation, instead of subjecting themselves to be under the yoke of law.

The Bible says that fulfilling the law of Christ is more important than that of the Old Testament laws, which is impossible to keep to their perfection. Paul emphasizes that none of us should boast in our own capacity to save ourselves by keeping the law; instead everyone should glorify in the provision the Lord made for us, and that is by accepting Lord Jesus Christ, whose marks were borne by not only Apostle Paul but all those, who believe in the efficacy of the blood of Lord Jesus Christ.

Paul's feels as if he was under the travail of child birth to explain to Galatians the difference between law and grace. It is indeed hard to be under the law to be saved from perishing. Instead believe that "grace" alone is the way for salvation.

We are saved by grace through faith. He calls Galatians as "my little children", and tries to explain to them about the implications in believing that keeping law and doing good works only would save them.

Galatians were under the erroneous belief that keeping the law and doing works can only save them from perishing. They desired to take pride in a list of rules that they prescribed for themselves and to keep them. They thought keeping God's laws to the perfection is possible by man and therefore, they made their own set of rules to keep God's law. However, none is found, nor can be found ever to be keeping God's law perfectly.

In other words, it renders a notion that man can earn his own salvation by keeping a set of rules, like being good and doing good works or climb thousands of steps on a hillock to reach their imaginary god in a temple, or sit in meditation under a tree for many days or years to understand God and follow Him. These things help men to be good men but would not secure salvation. Salvation is available free of cost, and that is as simple as confessing Jesus as Lord and by believing in heart that God raised Him from the dead on the third day.

Lord Jesus came down into this world to redeem us from the bondage of sin, and, therefore, took upon himself, our transgressions and died for our sake. The fruits of the Holy Spirit are love, joy, peace, long-suffering, gentleness, goodness, faith, Meekness, temperance. A saved man will have in him the Spirit of God and will have the fruits of the Holy Spirit.

However, possession of these good qualities without accepting Jesus as 'Lord' will not secure salvation and eternal life. The only way to have eternal life is to believe in the efficacy of the blood of Jesus Christ and accept the fact that he died in our stead on the cross and rose from the dead. He is seated at the right hand of the Majesty now, pleading on our behalf.

SECTION III

REPROACH FOR THE NAME OF CHRIST

If ye be reproached for the name of Christ, happy are ye; for the spirit of glory and of God rests upon you: on their part he is evil spoken of, but on your part he is glorified. (1 Peter 4:14)

CHAPTER 20

FIERY TRIALS AND PROVISION OF

SALVATION

"The next day he saw Jesus coming toward him, and said, 'Behold, the Lamb of God, who takes away the sin of the world! This is he of whom I said, 'after me comes a man who ranks before me, because he was before me' " John 1:29, 30

The children of Israel murmured over and over against the Almighty God while they were on their journey from Egypt to the Promised Land Canaan. God knew of their failures and warned them several times. He even chastised them in order that they may come back to Him.

"...they did not every man cast away the abominations of their eyes, neither did they forsake the idols of Egypt: then I said, I will pour out my fury upon them, to accomplish my anger against them in the midst of the land of Egypt" (Ezekiel 20:8)

Although God did miracles and delivered them from the bondage of slavery for 400 years in Egypt under Pharaoh, and led them through the wilderness by providing them heavenly 'manna' as their food, and protecting them during day by pillar of cloud, and during night by pillar of fire, leading them the way they should go, yet they angered the LORD by rebelling against Him (Exodus 13:21). They did not hearken unto God.

 The LORD sent fiery serpents among the children of Israel for speaking against Him and His servant Moses. The serpents bit them and many fell to the ground and were about lose their lives. However, when they repented of their rebellion against God and His servant, Moses, by requesting the latter to pray to God on behalf of them, he did intercede on behalf of them to the LORD.

The LORD God answered Moses' prayer. As per the commandment of God Moses made a serpent of brass, and put it upon a pole. Whoever of those bitten by serpents looked at the serpent of brass lived. (Numbers 21:8-10).

The rebellious people, who spoke against the LORD and against the servant of God, received compassion and grace from the Almighty God, who saved them from perishing. It is by obedience to the word of the LORD God that they looked at the brazen serpent and by doing so, they were saved. They obeyed God's commandment and their obedience was counted as righteousness for them.

God honored their obedience and faith and gave them life. John the Baptist, the forerunner of Jesus Christ, recollects this provision when he spoke about the Lord and the provision of salvation in John 3:14-15. He pointed to the Son of God, whom he identified as "the lamb of God", and said the Lord will save people from their sin.

"And as Moses lifted up the serpent in the wilderness, even so must the Son of man be lifted up: That whosoever believeth in him should not perish, but have eternal life" (John 3:14-15)

Jesus is our Lord, born of the Virgin Mary when the Holy Spirit came upon her and the power of the Most High overshadowed her. The Lord was also called the Son of Man. He dwelt among us in flesh.

"And the angel answered her, 'The Holy Spirit will come upon you, and the power of the Most High will overshadow you; therefore the child to be born will be called holy—the Son of God' ".

John the Baptist said that He must be lifted up just as the brazen serpent was lifted up in the wilderness in order that "whosoever believeth on him should not perish, but have eternal life" Jesus was lifted up on the cross and he died for us bearing our sin and He was raised to life from the dead on the third day.

We should, therefore, be looking unto Jesus who is the author and finisher of our faith. He endured the cross with joy despising shame. He died for our sake, rose from the dead on the third day, ascended into heaven, and seated on the right hand of the Father. Bible says that if a man is not born-again, he will not see the Kingdom of God. For everyone, who did not yet receive salvation, it is necessary, therefore, that one must receive Jesus as personal savior by faith in him. (Hebrews 1:3 and 12:2)

The Lord says: "Come unto me, all ye that labor and are heavy laden, and I will give you rest" (Matthew 11:28)

CHAPTER 21

LIVING FOR GOD

Seeing that you are living for God your former friends, with whom you reveled, and feasted or drunk in wild parties, would be surprised as to what dramatic change led you to isolate yourself from them. In fact, they would slander you and speak evil of you because you do not join with them in their worldly activities.

We would better realize one truth that they who live in lustful lives, and speak evil of Godly men, would stand before the Lord to account for all the wrongs that they have done not only for themselves but also to others.

God is the judge and His judgments are righteous. Inasmuch as God is not respecter of persons, no one can escape from His righteous judgments. It should be borne in mind that Gospel was preached to everyone, even for those who are dead now, and they had opportunity to repent of their sins.

No one can escape with excuses that they did not hear the Gospel. There is also responsibility on the part of every one to seek who God is, and what salvation is all about. God has given the entire humanity in every region, language, and climatic conditions to know about His creation, and learn about His character, and attributes. Therefore, no one is excusable saying one has not come to know about God.

"Because that which may be known of God is manifest in them; for God hath shewed it unto them. For the invisible things of him from the creation of the world are clearly seen, being understood by the things that are made, even his eternal power and Godhead; so that they are without excuse" (Romans 1:19-20)

Ultimately the end of the world has to happen and it will happen. It is imperative, therefore, for believers to live in unity and in deep love for one another. Believers should be earnest and disciplined in their prayers.

Love covers multitude of sins. Every endeavor should be made to see that visiting brethren in the Lord, should be treated well without grudging. According to the Scriptures, everyone has some gift or the other to serve the Lord, and as good stewards of the Lord, and in the manifold of grace of God, everyone should minister one's brothers, and sisters in the Lord.

Identify your gift that you received from the Lord, and serve one another. If you have the gift of speaking, then do speak as though God were speaking through you. If you have gift of helping others, then do it with all the health, strength and energy God gives you. In all things believers should see that the name of God is glorified through our Lord and Savior Jesus Christ. Praises, adorations and dominions be to the Lord forever and ever.

CHAPTER 22

LABOR PAINS IN CHILD BIRTH

"When a woman is giving birth, she has sorrow because her hour has come, but when she has delivered the baby, she no longer remembers the anguish, for joy that a human being has been born into the world" John 16:21

When Adam and Eve sinned in the Garden of Eden transgressing the command of God the ground was cursed for man, the serpent was cursed, and God said to woman that she will have labor pains in deliverance of the child. The woman's fiery trial starts with the terrible suffering and pain and finally ends in her deliverance of the child.

"And the LORD God said unto the serpent, Because thou hast done this, thou art cursed above all cattle, and above every beast of the field; upon thy belly shalt thou go, and dust shalt thou eat all the days of thy life: And I will put enmity between thee and the woman, and between thy seed and her seed; it shall bruise thy head, and thou shalt bruise his heel. Unto the woman he said, I will greatly multiply thy sorrow and thy conception; in sorrow thou shalt bring forth children; and thy desire shall be to thy husband, and he shall rule over thee. And unto Adam he said, Because thou hast hearkened unto the voice of thy wife, and hast eaten of the tree, of which I commanded thee, saying, Thou shalt not eat of it: cursed is the ground for thy sake; in sorrow shalt thou eat of it all the days of thy life; Thorns also and thistles shall it bring forth to thee; and thou shalt eat the herb of the field; In the sweat of thy face shalt thou eat bread, till thou return unto the ground; for out of it were thou taken: for dust thou art, and unto dust shalt thou return" (Genesis 3:14-19)

The same baby that causes pain for the mother brings great joy to the mother immediately the baby is born into the world. The pain, which mother experiences transforms into glory and the mother is greatly happy. It is not because the pain is replaced by glory but because the pain is transformed into glory.

Nevertheless, the child that comes into the world, if it is alive, will cry entering into the world. However, as the child grows into youth, the child is happy. The discussion is not about unforeseen circumstances, or unhealthy babies, but it is about what generally takes place.

The sorrow at the time of deliverance of the child would be unbearable, and yet there is deliverance, and the woman is saved from death in child bearing. While conceiving the child she has the knowledge of the pain that she would have to bear during deliverance, and yet she chooses to bear the child. When she is delivered of the child, her joy is not only greater than the labor pains that she suffers, but very soon she forgets the pain.

Lord Jesus was comparing the pain woman suffers in child bearing and deliverance to that of the oncoming suffering His disciples would have because of the death of the savior, and as He is taken up into heaven.

The suffering surely will pass away soon with the return of Lord Jesus Christ. All the concern, anxiety, fear and tribulations they have to undergo when the Lord is in heaven, would soon disappear and they would not have to suffer any more. Until then they are assigned to do the Lord's work on the earth.

The period of their suffering is as similar as the woman who suffers pain but her pain and anxiety of mind turns very quickly into ecstasy when she seen a child is born from her womb. The disciples were comforted by the Lord that He will be with them forever even unto the end of the earth.

"And Jesus came and spoke unto them, saying, all power is given unto me in heaven and in earth. Go ye therefore, and teach all nations, baptizing them in the name of the Father, and of the Son, and of the Holy Ghost: Teaching them to observe all things whatsoever I have commanded you: and, lo, I am with you always, even unto the end of the world. Amen" (Matthew 28:18-20)

"But ye shall receive power, after that the Holy Ghost is come upon you: and ye shall be witnesses unto me both in Jerusalem, and in all Judaea, and in Samaria, and unto the uttermost part of the earth. And when he had spoken these things, while they beheld, he was taken up; and a cloud received him out of their sight. And while they looked steadfastly toward heaven as he went up, behold, two men stood by them in white apparel; which also said, you men of Galilee, why stand ye gazing up into heaven? this same Jesus, which is taken up from you into heaven, shall so come in like manner as ye have seen him go into heaven" (Acts 1:8-11)

CHAPTER 23

BE WISE WHILE YOU PREACH

(Recent trend of preaching in India shows that many innocent preachers are landing in Jails besides being beaten up very badly. In the light of above, I felt it necessary to write this article).

"Submit yourselves to every ordinance of man for the Lord's sake: whether it be to the king, as supreme" (1 Peter 2:13)

"And Jesus came and spoke unto them, saying, all power is given unto me in heaven and in earth. Go ye therefore, and teach all nations, baptizing them in the name of the Father, and of the Son, and of the Holy Ghost: Teaching them to observe all things whatsoever I have commanded you: and, lo, I am with you always, even unto the end of the world. Amen" (Matthew 28:18-20)

"No man can come to me, except the Father which hath sent me draw him: and I will raise him up at the last day" (John 6:44)

Fight for your rights if you are not violating constitutional rights embedded in the law of the land with regard to freedom of speech, bearing in mind that your freedom is not an authorization to trample upon freedom of speech of others.

The last four verses of Matthew Chapter 9 show us that the preaching of the Gospel is so needed in those days. As Jesus was going down all the cities and villages, teaching in Jewish Synagogues, and proclaiming the good news of the kingdom of heaven, which was at hand, He saw multitudes of people craving for healing of their diseases.

The Lord was moved with compassion for them because they had no leader to look after them. He called His disciples, and said to them that harvest is plenty but workmen are few. He meant to say that those who are receptive of the Good news of the kingdom of heaven are plenty, but the Gospel preachers are few.

He then instructs them to approach the Lord of the harvest in order that he may put Gospel preachers at work. God is the proprietor of the harvest and He alone can send the workers to reap the harvest (cf. Matthew 9:35-38).

Lord Jesus then calls his twelve disciples and gives them the power against unclean spirits, to cast them out, and heal every kind of sickness and every manner of disease. The first and foremost instruction he gave was that they should not go in the way of gentiles or enter into the city of Samaritans, but go the lost sheep of Israel.

The first preference was to preach Gospel to the children of Israel, and then to Judea and Samaria and then to the uttermost parts of the world. There are two reasons why Jesus said to them to first to the house of Israel. The first and foremost reason was that they were chosen generation the covenanted people offspring of Jacob, whose father, Isaac, was the promised son of Abraham.

God had made unconditional covenant with Abraham that He will bless Abram's (later named as Abraham) offspring through Isaac, and not Ishmael, who was born to the handmaid of Sarai (later named as Sarah). The second reason was that all others were gentiles, especially those who were in Samaria, who were a mixture of people born to Jews and Gentiles.

Many Gentiles were settlements of those, who were brought into that region by Assyrians. Jews from Southern Kingdom of Israel treated them like 'dogs'. They did not want to get defiled by them. If the disciples went first to Gentiles to preach the Gospel, they would never had a chance to enter into Southern Kingdom of Israel.

Jesus was Jew and He gave all the preference for His own people first, and then to others. Was it tantamount to showing partiality? No! Because the children of Israel were chosen people of God from the time when the seed of Israel was in Abraham. That is why Jesus reiterated this preference after His resurrection and before His ascension into heaven as we read in Acts 1:8.

Jesus said to them that as they enter a city or town they should enquire as to who in that city is worthy where they can stay. When they find a man who is worthy to accommodate them, they should salute the people in that house and stay there.

The Lord says their peace will come upon that house. However, if someone does not accommodate them, or hear their words, they should shake off the dust of their feet. The Lord says Sodom and Gomorrah will be more tolerable at the time of judgment than that city which refused to accommodate them or hear Gospel from them.

Another important instruction Jesus gave them was to be wise like serpents, and harmless as doves when they are preaching good news to the people. They were being sent by the Lord as sheep into the midst of wolves.

The disciples of Jesus were innocent people not armed to fight with anyone, nor were they asked to confront anyone who opposed them. If people did not listen to their message they were asked to shake off the dust of their feet and leave the place and preach at another city.

The Lord assured them that they would not have finished their task of preaching in all the cities of house of Israel even if they hurried up catch up with their task. In other words, there is no meaning in staying at one place and fight to teach the Gospel; leave the place if the people of that place are unwilling to listen and go to another place to preach the Gospel.

In spite of being so careful the persecutions are inevitable. They come their way and Gospel preachers fall victim to persecutions, and when they fall victims of persecutions, as the Lord says, they need not be afraid of anything, but trust in the Lord, who will speak to the authorities through His Spirit. None of the authorities can destroy the soul of any believer. The believer should fear the Lord who can destroy not only their bodies, but also their souls.

According to the Lord, we do not need to invite persecution by intruding into private lives of people forcibly to preach the Gospel, but if persecution comes on to us by itself while preaching Gospel, the Lord will speak for us.

He said earlier "Happy those persecuted for righteousness' sake—because theirs is the reign of the heavens" (Matthew 5:10). The Lord says...

"And whenever they may persecute you in this city, flee to the other, for verily I say to you, ye may not have completed the cities of Israel till the Son of Man may come. (Matthew 10:23)

Finally, among many points mentioned in Matthew 10:1-42, four points are extremely important and noteworthy, especially in the present circumstances where innocent preachers, or helpers to preachers are getting into trouble.

1.   Preach Gospel of Jesus Christ (Matthew 10:5-10; Acts 1:8)

2.   Stay in city/town/home which is worthy and receptive (Ref. Matthew 10:13)

3.   If the city/town/home which is not worthy and not receptive, shake off the dust of your feet at that city/town/house, while you depart (Ref. Matthew 10:14-15)

4.   Persecutions are inevitable while preaching, but we do not need to stay at one place to be persecuted. When we are persecuted we are blessed, but the Lord did not say to us to stay at one place and preach even as the city/town/home/people refuse to hear the word of God. Rather, the Lord says, leave that place and go and preach at another place. The harvest is plenty but the laborers are few.

Some points that may be helpful for preachers in their localities in order not to get into trouble with authorities and land in Jail. Bear in mind what Lord Jesus said...

•   "No man can come to me, except the Father which hath sent me draw him: and I will raise him up at the last day" (John 6:44)

•   There are misconceptions in understanding these verses that preachers would think they can go into any private property and preach violating laws of the land.

•   "Go ye therefore, and teach all nations, baptizing them in the name of the Father, and of the Son, and of the Holy Ghost: Teaching them to observe all things whatsoever I have commanded you: and, lo, I am with you always, even unto the end of the world. Amen" (Matthew 28:19-20) and John 14:6; Acts 4:6-7; Acts 4:18; Acts 4:19 without realizing that those conversations were with religious leaders. Of course, in Acts

5:27-29 they were before Sanhedrin. The word "Sanhedrin" traces back to Numbers 11:16 where it says...

•   "And the LORD said unto Moses, Gather unto me seventy men of the elders of Israel, whom thou knows to be the elders of the people, and officers over them; and bring them unto the tabernacle of the congregation, that they may stand there with thee" (Numbers 11:16).

•   In ancient Israel the Sanhedrin was equal to present Supreme Court in our land. Much later after Peter and John preached and faced interrogations, "Sanhedrin" was dissolved by Roman Government. During the days of Jesus Sanhedrin tried Him, and several illegal decisions were taken (ref. John 18:12-14, 19-23).

It is imperative that we consider what Peter and Paul spoke about obeying the law of the land.

Peter says...

"Submit yourselves to every ordinance of man for the Lord's sake: whether it be to the king, as supreme; Or unto governors, as unto them that are sent by him for the punishment of evildoers, and for the praise of them that do well. For so is the will of God, that with well doing ye may put to silence the ignorance of foolish men: As free, and not using your liberty for a cloak of maliciousness, but as the servants of God. Honor all men. Love the brotherhood. Fear God. Honor the king. (1 Peter 2:13-17)

Paul says...

"Let every soul be subject unto the higher powers. For there is no power but of God: the powers that be are ordained of God. Whosoever therefore resists the power, resists the ordinance of God: and they that resist shall receive to themselves damnation.

For rulers are not a terror to good works, but to the evil. Wilt thou then not be afraid of the power? Do that which is good, and thou shalt have praise of the same: For he is the minister of God to thee for good. But if thou do that which is evil, be afraid; for he bears not the sword in vain: for he is the minister of God, a revenger to execute wrath upon him that doeth evil. Wherefore ye must needs be subject, not only for wrath, but also for conscience sake. For this cause pay ye tribute also: for they are God's ministers, attending continually upon this very thing. Render therefore to all their dues: tribute to whom tribute is due; custom to whom custom; fear to whom fear; honor to whom honor" (Romans 13:1-7)

It is quite evident that Bible does not teach indiscipline. Can we intentionally disobey the laws of the land? No. Not at all!

According to Bible as long as the law of the land does not contradict the law of God we are bound to obey the law of the land, but when the law of the land contradicts the law of God we are supposed to obey the law of God; nevertheless, we cannot do anything without accepting Government's authority over us. This is evident the way Peter and John submitted themselves to flogging. They rejoiced in obeying God. We should bear in mind that we do have some rights to exercise to preach the Gospel. It is by doing in disciplined way.

Some points to be borne in mind while preaching in local areas.

•   Obtain permission from Government before preaching in areas where Government has strictly restricted. We cannot sneak into private properties and preach Gospel where soliciting is not permitted. What is Government refuses permission? Do not preach there. It is as simple as obeying God's command that shake off your dust of your feet at that city/town/people, and go to another place and preach Gospel of Jesus Christ there.

God is not going to ask an account from us for not preaching in prohibited areas.

• We cannot use public address system unless permitted by Government

• We cannot preach during night times.

• Preach from Public property

• We cannot disturb peace in an area where we preach

• We cannot loiter.

Circumstances and instructions vary from place to place. We should have clear knowledge of the law of the land, rules and regulations of that area where we preach. Many preachers violate the law of the land misinterpreting instructions and provisions in the Bible, inviting for themselves serious problems.

"I exhort therefore, that, first of all, supplications, prayers, intercessions, and giving of thanks, be made for all men; For kings, and for all that are in authority; that we may lead a quiet and peaceable life in all godliness and honesty. For this is good and acceptable in the sight of God our Saviour; who will have all men to be saved, and to come unto the knowledge of the truth. For there is one God, and one mediator between God and men, the man Christ Jesus; who gave himself a ransom for all, to be testified in due time" (1 Timothy 2:1-6)

CHAPTER 24

THE LORD IS OUR DELIVERER

"I waited patiently for the LORD; and he inclined unto me, and heard my cry. He brought me up also out of a horrible pit, out of the miry clay, and set my feet upon a rock, and established my goings. And he hath put a new song in my mouth, even praise unto our God: many shall see it, and fear, and shall trust in the LORD"

(Psalms 40:1-3)

An affluent man or one in his prime youth does seldom think of devoting his precious time to honor his Maker, the Almighty God. As long as his blood runs hot in his arteries he seeks to fulfill his heart's desire of enjoying the worldly pleasures and passions. However a time comes when he would realize that he is struck with some serious disease as a consequence of immoral life, and then he seeks to find peace and tranquility and to add to it forgiveness from God.

King David's life was no exception to such passions that ran high in his early days of his kingship, and he felt the pinch of it, as he describes in Psalm 38, when he was struck with an unknown disease.

"For mine iniquities are gone over mine head: as a heavy burden they are too heavy for me. My wounds stink and are corrupt because of my foolishness" (Psalms 38:4-5)

David committed sin and sank into deep mire clog, a slippery ground, where he could not stand firm, and from there he slipped again into deep waters (symbolic of deep troubles). He realized that he committed blunders in his life, and then, prayed to God to deliver him, not only from the troubles he was in, but also from those who hated him.

While he was in great trouble, and as he prayed, the LORD delivered him from his troubles, and placed him on a rock of safety, securing his feet firmly. He felt as if he was in a miry clog in a cistern to be destroyed just as Joseph was put in cistern by his brothers before he was sold into the hands of Midianites. Jeremiah the prophet, who came nearly 300 years after David, also suffered a similar imprisonment in the cistern on false charges (cf. Jeremiah 38:6).

It was usual in those days to confine the offenders to cisterns where there was no water but mire. One, who is delivered out of such miserable condition, knows the importance of freedom, and expresses gratitude to the LORD who delivered him. This kind of confinement was too harsh for anyone to tolerate, especially to David, and he feels so comfortable when the LORD delivered him from the cistern, where he was stuck in mire clog.

He waited patiently for the LORD, and the LORD came near to Him and heard his cry. The LORD drew him up from the pit of destruction and out of miry clog and set his feet upon a rock and made his steps secure.

As his feet were secured on a rock he sings a new song, which the LORD placed in his mouth, a song of praise to our God, as a reward for waiting patiently on Him. His life of singing, praising, and honoring the LORD, was exemplary for many who would fear the LORD and put their trust in Him.

Waiting on the LORD will not go in vain. All things work for good for those, who cast their burden on the Lord, for Him to take care and trust Him. Psalmist advises us to be of good courage and as we develop to have good courage in Him He strengthens our hearts and speaks to us in our hearts revealing what is good and what is not.

Rest in the Lord and wait patiently on Him. Do not worry seeing the heathen prosper in their ways that might be a pursuit to accumulate wealth in wrong ways. The wrong pursuit of gaining wealth and pleasures of this world may appear to be good for a short while, but the end thereof would be very bad.

As the children of God, we are not here to gain wealth, prosperity and secular power. Gather treasures in heaven, where moth does not corrupt our possessions, and where our possessions last forever.

Psalmist, therefore, prays to the LORD to hear his cry in order that peace may not be withheld from favoring him. He acknowledges that he is a stranger in this world, and a sojourner as were his forefathers. His faith in the LORD was great. He says the LORD hid him in his pavilion, when he was in times of troubles, and he believed that in the secret place of LORD's tabernacle did He hide him, and thereafter set him upon a rock. He knew that the steps of the good man were ordered by the LORD and therefore, his delight was to follow the LORD's ways.

David, having found solace in the LORD and having being delivered from troubles advises all of us to sing to the LORD a new song, and play skillfully musical instruments with loud noise. He says the righteous will laugh at the wicked and fear the LORD.

Blessed is the one who trusts the LORD and does not turn to the proud, and to those who go astray after a lie. Honor the Son of God, lest He would be angry and you perish from the way. Blessed are all those who fear Him and put their trust in Him.

Make a decision today that you would not set a wicked thing before your eyes. Those, who turn aside from the LORD, are hateful to the righteous, and the righteous will not cleave to them.

(cf. Psalms 2:12; 27:5, 14; 33:3; 37:7, 23; 39:12, 52:6, 7;69:2; 69:14; 101:3)

CHAPTER 25

SUFFERING FOR THE RIGHT CAUSE

"For we have not an high priest which cannot be touched with the feeling of our infirmities; but was in all points tempted like as we are, yet without sin" (Hebrews 4:15)

It is no wonder that almost everyone knows that there is a great difference between suffering for the right cause and suffering for criminal activities. Suffering for illegal causes and feeling sorry over such actions would not absolve one from being punished in this world, or in the world to come.

Fiery trials come in our way when we suffer for the sake of righteousness. We are tested and the tests may be so severe that we might even reach a stage when we feel it is too hard to endure anymore. However, scripture calls for our endurance through persecutions and suffering without giving up. Lord Jesus had overcome the world and we are encouraged that we also can overcome fiery trials and temptations.

Blessed are we when we suffer persecutions for His name sake. It should be beyond our thoughts that persecutions happen only to us. Rather we should know that persecutions are universal and can trouble anyone in the world. Persecutions are more for the believers in Christ. They are forced to give up their faith in the Lord.

Persecutors may bring forth enormous damage on those who suffer persecutions. We should not think, in such circumstances that some strange thing is happening to us. Suffering as a result of persecution is not only here in New Testament period, but it was also there in the Old Testament period, as well.

Great prophets like Isaiah, Jeremiah, and the disciples of Jesus Christ suffered persecutions. They all have suffered persecutions for the sake of exalting the name of our LORD.

Moses, the servant of God, suffered persecution at the hands of children of Israel, who murmured all through their journey for forty years, yet he did not give up serving the Lord.

The failure on his part was because he overstepped God's command. As scriptures show us Matthew 17:3 Moses and Elijah appeared to three disciples who were with Lord Jesus Christ during the Lord's transfiguration.

Shadrach, Meshach and Abednego disobeyed king Nebuchadnezzar's command that everyone in the land of Babylon should make an obeisance to the image of Nebuchadnezzar when they hear the 'the voice of the cornet, the flute, the harp, the sackbut, the psaltery, the symphony, and all kinds of music'.

On receipt of complaints that Shadrach, Meshach and Abednego did not make obeisance to the golden image king Nebuchadnezzar raised, he ordered that they be thrown into a furnace of fire that was made seven times hotter than usual temperature.

Mighty men who threw them into the fiery furnace got burnt up and died instantly, but Shadrach, Meshach and Abednego not only survived the heat of the hot furnace but there was a fourth man in the furnace guarding them. The fourth one was none other than the pre-incarnate Jesus.

Nebuchadnezzar saw the fourth man and said…"Lo, I am seeing four men loose, walking in the midst of the fire, and they have no hurt; and the appearance of the fourth is like to a son of the gods." Then Nebuchadnezzar hath drawn near to the gate of the burning fiery furnace; he hath answered and said, `Shadrach, Meshach, and Abed-Nego, servants of God Most High come forth, yea, come;' then come forth do Shadrach, Meshach, and Abed-Nego, from the midst of the fire (cf. Daniel 3:1-30)

When such persecutions come in our way and we suffer, we have great hope in Lord Jesus Christ that He will sustain us, and bring the suffering to pass beyond us, in a pleasing way. It may be ending up in giving up life for His name sake, in which case we will have our rewards in heaven.

Surely it is great to gather treasures in heaven rather than great wealth on the earth. None of us will carry any of our possessions, wealth etc. when we leave this earth. Rejoice in the Lord that many God's people, and His servants have all suffered for upholding His name. If we are reproached for the name of our Lord Jesus Christ, happy are we, because the Spirit of God and His glory rests upon us.

On the contrary, let no one who suffers as a consequence of wrong doing, or involving in criminal activities, think that God will grant them any rewards. One, who suffer as a murderer, or as thief, or an evil-doer, or those, or who pursues after others' matters, reap consequences.

The consequences of their suffering would be because of their unlawful activities, which are not from God. Unlawful activities are not surely for rejoicing and, therefore, their suffering is not for the right cause. God is not going to endorse such activities as for Him, nor will He bless such an ones, who pursue illegal activities.

No doubt Satan will tempt believers into wrongful causes and if any believer yields to his temptation, he will point their failings and subject them to mockery and punishments rather than appreciating them. Satan is a great cheater. Many times he comes as an angel of light. Believer needs to be very cautious against the temptations of Satan.

Believers in the Lord should be strong in faith and depend upon Lord Jesus Christ to help come out of temptations. Bible says...

"There hath no temptation taken you but such as is common to man: but God is faithful, who will not suffer you to be tempted above that ye are able; but will with the temptation also make a way to escape, that ye may be able to bear it" (1 Corinthians 10:13)

God says no temptation is beyond any man's capacity to bear it, and the Lord will not only show us to get out of trouble, but He also provides a way out for us to get out of temptations.

We have a High Priest, who knows we are made of dust, because as He was an incarnate God on earth suffered the temptation from Satan, and had overcome them. The Lord defeated Satan at the cross of Calvary.

Our sin was judged at the cross, and therefore, there is nothing that we could be judged of. There is, of course, one kind of judgment believers will go through and it is at that "Judgement seat of Christ", also known as "Bema Seat" where believers will be rewarded for their work for the Lord, and for expansion of His kingdom. They are not going to be judged for condemnation. There is no condemnation for those who are in Him.

"For such an high priest became us, who is holy, harmless, undefiled, separate from sinners, and made higher than the heavens" (Hebrews 7:26)

"Now of the things which we have spoken this is the sum: We have such a high priest, who is set on the right hand of the throne of the Majesty in the heavens" (Hebrews 8:1)

We might think that our suffering for the sake of our Lord is great and unbearable, but it is not. In such circumstances when we feel our suffering is greater than we can bear, let us think of those, who will face unbearable sufferings, during great tribulation period.

It is so comforting to note that when we will be with the Lord, and they will be on earth, left behind to face such great troubles that no one has ever faced. Those problems that heathen and pagan face during great tribulation period are beyond our comprehension. They are beyond the capacity of heathen and pagan, who refused to obey Lord Jesus Christ. It is at that time that every knee that refused accept Him as Lord will fall at His feet and call on His name, and acknowledge that He is Lord (cf. 1 Peter 4:12-19)

CHAPTER 26

PERSECUTIONS

Persecutions exist not only in the New Testament period but they existed in the Old Testament period as well. The greatest persecution found in the Old Testament period was of the killing of prophets by the Jezebel, who was the wicked wife, of King Ahab.

"For it was so, when Jezebel cut off the prophets of the LORD, that Obadiah took an hundred prophets, and hid them by fifty in a cave, and fed them with bread and water" (1 Kings 18:4)

"Was it not told my lord what I did when Jezebel slew the prophets of the LORD, how I hid an hundred men of the LORD'S prophets by fifty in a cave, and fed them with bread and water?" (1 Kings 18:13)

King Manasseh did evil in the sight of the LORD.

"And he made his son pass through the fire, and observed times, and used enchantments, and dealt with familiar spirits and wizards: he wrought much wickedness in the sight of the LORD, to provoke him to anger. And he set a graven image of the grove that he had made in the house, of which the LORD said to David, and to Solomon his son, In this house, and in Jerusalem, which I have chosen out of all tribes of Israel, will I put my name forever: (2 Kings 21:6-7)

"And also for the innocent blood that he shed: for he filled Jerusalem with innocent blood; which the LORD would not pardon" (2 Kings 24:4)

Lord Jesus Christ said...

"Blessed are they which are persecuted for righteousness' sake: for theirs is the kingdom of heaven" (Matthew 5:10)

When John came neither eating nor drinking people said he has a devil, and when the Son of man came eating and drinking they said He was "gluttonous, and winebibber, a friend of publicans and sinners". Man has tongue and he talks; evil man condemns the righteous either way.

"For John came neither eating nor drinking, and they say, He hath a devil. The Son of man came eating and drinking, and they say, Behold a man gluttonous, and a winebibber, a friend of publicans and sinners. But wisdom is justified of her children" (Matthew 11:18-19)

Jesus never said the lives of the children of God will be pleasant and rid of troubles, trials and persecutions; rather He said that those who would not endure tribulations and persecutions have no root in themselves and, therefore, they are offended. He said blessed are those who suffer persecution for righteousness' sake.

"And he hath not root in himself, but is temporary, and persecution or tribulation having happened because of the word, immediately he is stumbled" (Matthew 13:21 YLT)

A great deal of the nature of persecutions Christians suffer and the blessings they received/or will receive by suffering is found in Mark 10:30 Acts 8:1; Acts 13:50; Romans 8:35 2; Corinthians 12:10 2; Thessalonians 1:4; 2 Timothy 3:11; Matthew 7:1; Luke 9:54-56; Romans 14:4; James 4:11, 12.

Saul, who persecuted the Church and later was known by the name "Paul", said...

"Who shall separate us from the love of Christ? Shall tribulation, or distress, or persecution, or famine, or nakedness, or peril, or sword?" (Romans 8:35)

Jesus spoke to Pharisees and Scribes and said to them that their fathers persecuted prophets and they were no better than them. He said that they were getting ready to slay the Messiah and His messengers and to reap the punishment by doing so. Surely as He said their enemies overtook them later as the history reveals. They have upon their heads the curse of killing Abel unto the blood of Zacharias.

"That upon you may come all the righteous blood shed upon the earth, from the blood of righteous Abel unto the blood of Zacharias son of Barachias, whom ye slew between the temple and the altar" (Matthew 23:35)

Jesus said to His disciples that if the world hated Him and persecuted Him, they will not be reluctant to persecute them as well.

"Remember the word that I said unto you, the servant is not greater than his lord. If they have persecuted me, they will also persecute you; if they have kept my saying, they will keep yours also" (John 15:20)

SECTION IV

PRIVILEGES OF GENTILES

Wherefore let them that suffer according to the will of God commit the keeping of their souls to him in well doing, as unto a faithful Creator. (1 Peter 4:19)

CHAPTER 27

GENTILES SHALL SEE HIS

RIGHTEOUSNESS

And the Gentiles shall see thy righteousness, and all kings thy glory: and thou shalt be called by a new name, which the mouth of the LORD shall name (Isaiah 62:2)

Lord Jesus Christ, who is the messiah, says that He will not sit quite, nor will He rest until He redeems the city of Jerusalem. He has set watchmen upon the walls of Jerusalem and they will not keep quite nor will sleep but keep a watch over the city and will make the city a praise of the earth.

This is a promise of Messiah and He has sworn by His right hand and by the arm of His strength. He promised that none of the enemies of Jerusalem will eat its corn as their food no stranger will ever drink its wine. Gentiles will see its righteousness.

Lord Jesus Christ defeats the kings loyal to Antichrist at 'Armageddon', and sits on the throne of David and reigns for a thousand years. In the thousand years of His rule there shall be perfect peace.

Satan will be bound with chains and thrown into abyss by an angel who comes from heaven. Later Satan will be released for a short time when he goes Gog and Magog to deceive the nations but fire from God comes down from heaven and devours Satan. (Revelation Ch. 20:8)

The dead who did not accept Jesus Christ as their personal savior will resurrect at that time. The Lord shall judge them at the 'Great white throne' and cast them along with death, hell, and the devil and his angels into the 'lake of fire' to be tormented for ever and ever.

This is the second death. For those who are saved, there is no second death but they will have everlasting life to be with the Lord for ever and ever. Note here when Antichrist and false prophet are thrown into the lake of fire! It is before the devil that deceived!!! Revelation 20:10 confirms it.

When the devil was cast into the lake of fire, the Antichrist and the false prophet were already there in the lake of fire. These are only the ones who will be in the lake of fire before the 'Great White Throne Judgment' (Revelation 16:16 and Revelation 20:8-10). Does the Scripture say any body is thrown into the lake of fire before Antichrist and false prophet? No, not at all!

There shall come out of heaven a New Jerusalem and we, who are saved, shall be in that Holy City. The Church is the bride of our Lord Jesus Christ and will be with Him for ever and ever reigning along with Him and every individual having been conformed to His image, irrespective of their earthly affiliation, while they were on the earth, to Jews or Gentiles.

CHAPTER 28

ROYAL PRIESTHOOD

"But ye are a chosen generation, a royal priesthood, an holy nation, a peculiar people; that ye should shew forth the praises of him who hath called you out of darkness into his marvelous light" (1 Peter 2:9)

1 Peter 2:9 lists the position of believers in the sight of our living God. Believers in Christ are a chosen generation, a royal priesthood, and holy nation, a peculiar people and then it lists the responsibilities of believer towards the One who has given such status before him. God called us from out of darkness into marvelous light in order that we may worship him, praise him and bear a good testimony for him.

The priests in the Old Testament period were required to offer sacrifices for themselves and then for the congregation which they were heading.

It differed as the times changed and the way they offered sacrifices varied in different time periods.

Until the Mosaic Law came into existence individual Saints in the Old Testament offered

Sacrifices all by themselves that entitled them to be called as Priests; and after the Law was proposed the entire congregations of the children of Israel were called the "Kingdom of Priests", but because they violated the Law the priestly office was confined to the tribe of Levi.

Aaron and his sons became the Priests. The Priest in the Old Testament period could enter the Most Holy Place in the Tabernacle only once a year.

There are at least four individuals who can be taken for consideration. (1) Noah (2) Abraham (3) Isaac and (4) Jacob

Noah built an altar unto the Lord and offered clean beast, and clean fowl as burnt offerings on the altar. (Genesis 8:20) Abraham took two of his young men with him and Isaac his son and went to offer the burnt offering. (Genesis 22:3)

Isaac built an altar and called upon the name of the Lord, and pitched his tent and his servants dug a well (Genesis 26:25).

Jacob offered sacrifice upon the mount and called his brothers to eat bread and they ate the bread. (Genesis 31:54)

Then after the Law was proposed the children of Israel as a whole nation was called "kingdom of priests" (Exodus 19:6)

But they violated the Law and antagonized God several times. They worshipped Idols and angered God. Then, God confined priesthood to the Tribe of Levi. Aaron and his sons from the Tribe of Levi were the priests. (Exodus 28:1)

"And hath made us kings and priests unto God and his Father; to him be glory and dominion for ever and ever. Amen". (Revelation 1:6)

This shows the priesthood of individual believers in the present age.

The sons of Aaron were anointed. They had on them Ephod, which is a linen apron, bonnet, which is a cap, breastplate, which is a metal piece worn around the body as a defensive armor, and miter which is a head-band used as a turban.

The stipulations God prescribed for priests were so stringent that they could not violate any of the conditions that God prescribed. These details are mentioned in Exodus Ch. 27, 28 and 29

Lord Jesus Christ was not after the order of Aaron but he was after the order of Melchizedek.

While the priesthood of Aaron was limited; the priesthood of Melchizedek is for ever and ever. Even though there are not many references about Melchizedek, yet the references that are found in Genesis 14:18, Psalm 110:4, Hebrews 5:6 and in Hebrews Chapter 7 give us great knowledge about Lord Jesus Christ's Priesthood after the order of Melchizedek. Jesus is Priest, Prophet and King. Jesus became our High Priest because he offered himself as a sacrifice for our sins.

"For every high priest taken from among men is ordained for men in things pertaining to God, that he may offer both gifts and sacrifices for sins" (Hebrews 5:1)

"But into the second went the high priest alone once every year, not without blood, which he offered for himself, and for the errors of the people" (Hebrews 9:7)

"By a new and living way, which he hath consecrated for us, through the veil, that is to say, his flesh" (Hebrews 10:20)

Having therefore, brethren, boldness to enter into the holiest by the blood of Jesus, By a new and living way, which he hath consecrated for us, through the veil, that is to say, his flesh; And having an high priest over the house of God; Let us draw near with a true heart in full assurance of faith, having our hearts sprinkled from an evil conscience, and our bodies washed with pure water. (Hebrews 10:19-22)

According to Levite Priesthood a Priest could not be king and likewise a King could not be a Priest. That is the reason why we see King Saul was not accepted by God as Priest.

"And Saul said, Bring hither a burnt offering to me, and peace offerings. And he offered the burnt offering". (1 Samuel 13:9)

The result was seen in 1 Samuel 13:13

"And Samuel said to Saul, Thou hast done foolishly: thou hast not kept the commandment of the LORD thy God, which he commanded thee: for now would the LORD have established thy kingdom upon Israel forever". (1 Samuel 13:13)

Melchizedek king of Salem was not of the order of Levite. Abraham gave him tithe to Melchizedek.

"And Melchizedek king of Salem brought forth bread and wine: and he was the priest of the most high God. And he blessed him, and said, blessed be Abram of the most high God, possessor of heaven and earth: And blessed be the most high God, which hath delivered thine enemies into thy hand. And he gave him tithes of all". (Genesis 14:18-20)

"For this Melchisedec, king of Salem, priest of the most high God, who met Abraham returning from the slaughter of the kings, and blessed him" (Hebrews 7:1)

When Jesus was crucified the veil in the temple was rent into two from top to bottom signifying granting to us access to the Father through the Son of God, who is our High Priest. There is, therefore, no more a Priest required for us to offer sacrifices on our behalf nor are we required to confess our sins to any Priest in this world in order that he may convey to God our sins to be forgiven. We are all priests and he has given us the status of "Royal Priesthood" and Lord Jesus Christ is our High Priest and mediator. (Matthew 27:51)

"But Christ being come an high priest of good things to come, by a greater and more perfect tabernacle, not made with hands, that is to say, not of this building" (Hebrews 9:11)

We are given responsibility to offer sacrifices and those sacrifices are presenting our bodies as living sacrifice, holy and acceptable unto God. (Romans 12:1).

We should be ready to help our brethren (1 John 3:16). We should visit the fatherless and widows in their affliction, and keep ourselves without any blemish. (James 1:27).

We should offer sacrifices of praises and thanks to God continually. (Hebrews 13:15)

"I exhort therefore, that, first of all, supplications, prayers, intercessions, and giving of thanks, be made for all men". (1 Timothy 2:1)

CHAPTER 29

LAMB OF GOD

In the New Testament John identified Lord Jesus as the "Lamb of God", who takes away the sin of the world.

"The next day he saw Jesus coming toward him, and said, 'Behold, the Lamb of God, who takes away the sin of the world! This is he of whom I said, 'after me comes a man who ranks before me, because he was before me' " John 1:29, 30

The typology of the slaying of the Lamb for the redemption of the children of Israel from the bondage of slavery is fulfilled when Lord Jesus Christ was crucified on the cross of Calvary for the redemption of mankind. Whoever believes in Jesus as Savior will have salvation free of cost and whoever rejects Him as savior will perish according to John 3:16 John the Baptist pointed to Lord Jesus Christ and identified Him as the "Lamb of God."

"The next day John sees Jesus coming unto him, and saith, Behold the Lamb of God, which taketh away the sin of the world" John 1:29

The Passover Lamb was set aside on the tenth day of the first month of Jewish calendar i.e. the month of "Abib" and was slain on fourteenth day of the month (Ref. Exodus 12:1-6).

The children of Israel applied the blood of the lamb to the lintel posts of the doors of their houses in order that the Lord may Passover that home without killing the first born in the house. The firstborn of the Egyptians including that of Pharaoh was killed by the Lord and then Pharaoh released the children of Israel from the bondage of slavery. "And it came to pass, that at midnight the LORD smote all the firstborn in the land of Egypt, from the firstborn of Pharaoh that sat on his throne unto the firstborn of the captive that was in the dungeon; and all the firstborn of cattle" (Exodus 12:29)

Apostle John saw in his vision as recorded in Revelation Chapter 19:13 that Lord Jesus Christ was clothed with vesture dipped in blood.

"And he [was] clothed with vesture dipped in blood: and his name is called The Word of God" Revelation 19:13 and His name was "The Word of God".

"In the beginning was the Word, and the Word was with God, and the Word was God" (John 1:1)

The Word was made flesh and lived among us.

"And the Word was made flesh, and dwelt among us, (and we beheld his glory, the glory as of the only begotten of the Father,) full of grace and truth" (John 1:14)

Thus we see three important truths about Lord Jesus Christ.

HE IS THE LAMB OF GOD

HIS VESTURE WAS DIPPED IN BLOOD

HIS NAME IS THE WORD OF GOD

SECTION V   LIFE AFTER DEATH

"O death, where is thy sting? O grave, where is thy victory?" (1 Corinthians 15:55)

"For the Lord himself shall descend from heaven with a shout, with the voice of the archangel, and with the trump of God: and the dead in Christ shall rise first: Then we which are alive and remain shall be caught up together with them in the clouds, to meet the Lord in the air: and so shall we ever be with the Lord" (1 Thessalonians 4:16-17)

At the appearance of Lord Jesus Christ again, the dead, who had repented of their sins, and confessed Jesus as Lord and believed in heart that Lord Jesus was raised by God on the third day, will rise from the dead and look at their graves and say "O grave where is thy victory", and likewise, those who are alive at that time, and had repented of their sins, and confessed Jesus as Lord, and believed in their heart that Lord Jesus was raised from the dead, will be caught up to meet the Lord in the air, and then look at the death and say "O death, where is thy sting"?

Thus the death and grave are overcome by the believers in Christ, just as the Lord overcame the death. The risen ones will have glorified bodies. There will be no pain and no suffering in eternity for those, who believed in Lord Jesus Christ as their Savior. They will all live happily with the Lord Jesus Christ forever and ever.

CHAPTER 30

DEATH AND LIFE AFTER DEATH

It was when Adam and Eve sinned that Satan gained power over death, which remained in his domain. It is evident from the words of Jesus that Satan has his own kingdom and demons are as his followers. (Cf. Matthew 12:24-27)

God commanded the man (Adam) saying to him that he may freely eat of every tree of the garden but shall not eat of the tree of the knowledge of good and evil. The wages of transgression of God's command was that he shall surely die in the day he eats thereof. (Genesis 2:16-17).

God made woman out of one of the ribs of man and she became man's wife. Adam and Eve lived happily until sin entered their lives through the deception by serpent who enticed Eve to eat from the forbidden tree. She not only ate the fruit from the forbidden tree but she gave it to man also and thus they became enemies to God.

Later God visited them and pronounced punishments on Serpent, Adam and Eve. Serpent was cursed and the ground was cursed for man and God said that woman will bear children in pain. God clothed Adam and Eve with coats of skin signifying that God made a way for their reconciliation (Genesis 3:1-21).

JESUS REBUKED PHARISEES

"Ye are of your father the devil, and the lusts of your father ye will do. He was a murderer from the beginning, and abode not in the truth, because there is no truth in him. When he speaketh a lie, he speaketh of his own: for he is a liar, and the father of it". (John 8:44)

Before the Mosaic Law was given Adam transgressed. Cain killed Abel. Wickedness prevailed during Noah's period and Lot's period. God did not allow them to go without penalty but punished them. Apostle Paul wrote in Romans Chapter 5 about sin and death.

"Wherefore, as by one man sin entered into the world, and death by sin; and so death passed upon all men, for that all have sinned: (For until the law sin was in the world: but sin is not imputed when there is no law. Nevertheless death reigned from Adam to Moses, even over them that had not sinned after the similitude of Adam's transgression, who is the figure of him that was to come. But not as the offence, so also is the free gift. For if through the offence of one many be dead, much more the grace of God, and the gift by grace, which is by one man, Jesus Christ, hath abounded unto many. And not as it was by one that sinned, so is the gift: for the judgment was by one to condemnation, but the free gift is of many offences unto justification. For if by one man's offence death reigned by one; much more they which receive abundance of grace and of the gift of righteousness shall reign in life by one, Jesus Christ.)" (Romans 5:12-17, Cf. also Romans 6:23)

Notice the phrase "nevertheless death reigned from Adam to Moses..." The death had power on man even before the written law was given.

 "Whosoever commits sin transgresses also the law: for sin is the transgression of the law". (1 John 3:4)

The transgression of law is sin. Does it mean that it is applicable only from the time Mosaic Law was given? No. God's law prevailed even before the written law was given. Man was governed under Conscience and God punished sin even before the written law was given. The death reigned from Adam to Moses even when there was no written law, and death continued to have its power on sinner.

THE STING OF DEATH

"O death, where is thy sting? O grave, where is thy victory?" (1 Corinthians 15:55)

Scripture asks the death as to where its sting is? Sin causes death but that death is defeated by Jesus. In other words Satan, who is the author of sin, has the power to cause the death of a sinner. If we are without Sin, then death has no power over us; but Scripture says all have sinned and come short of the glory of God. If we say have not sinned we are liars and we make God a liar.

"For all have sinned and short of the glory of God (Romans 3:23)

"If we say that we have not sinned, we make him a liar, and his word is not in us". (1 John 1:10)

The Scripture says that we shall not all sleep, but we shall all be changed. When Lazarus was dead for four days Jesus saw him and said "Our friend Lazarus sleeps..." The disciples of Jesus took his saying at face value and thought Lazarus was, indeed, sleeping. However, Jesus spoke of the death of Lazarus and said he is dead. Jesus said that He will wake him up from his sleep, indicating that He will raise Lazarus. Martha believed and said to Jesus that she knew Lazarus would rise in the resurrection at the last day. But then, Jesus said He is the resurrection. (Cf. John: 11:13, 14, 24, 25)

"Jesus said unto her, I am the resurrection, and the life: he that believeth in me, though he were dead, yet shall he live" (John 11:25)

The departure of Lazarus from this earth was painful to Mary and Martha, who were sisters of Lazarus. How comforting it is to note that Jesus shares the grief of his followers and redeems them from their grief. Jesus was their good friend and shared their grief

"Jesus wept". (John 11:35)

Jesus raised Lazarus from his death and this was after four days had lapsed after his death. Many Jews believed in Jesus and some of them left that place to tell Pharisees about the resurrection of Lazarus that they saw. However, the resurrection of believers in Christ, when Christ shall come again is different from the resurrection of Lazarus, who was raised to console Mary and Martha and this miracle was one of the many miracles that Jesus did during his public ministry on this earth.

God can extend the life of a person on this earth at his discretion. Hezekiah's life was extended by fifteen years when he prayed; but there came a day when he died. (2 Kings 20:6, 2 Kings 20:21. Isaiah 38:5).

The resurrection of believers in Christ when Christ shall come again will be in the changing of corruptible bodies to incorruptible bodies in the twinkling of an eye. Apostle Paul described it in 1 Corinthians 15:51-57 where he wrote that it was a mystery that was revealed. He wrote that we shall not all sleep but will be changed and in a moment, in the twinkling of an eye, at the last trump, when our corruptible bodies will put on incorruptible bodies and rise to immortality.

The sting of death, which is sin, and the strength of sin, which is the law, puts man to death, but the death is swallowed up in victory for the believers in Christ. God gives victory over death through Lord Jesus Christ. It is in this context that he said: "O death, where is thy sting? O grave, where is thy victory?" (1 Corinthians 15:55)

There is salvation to rise from death to everlasting life. It is by confessing our sins to Jesus and by accepting Him as our personal savior. The strength of sin is the law, which points our guilt, but does not save us from Sin. It is only the blood of Lord Jesus Christ that can cleanse us from our Sin. It is only by grace through faith in Jesus that we are saved and not by any good works. Jesus forgives us of our sins and trespasses no matter how grave they are.

When Jesus was on this earth he never saw any one die in his presence. He saw the dead and He raised them to life. Lazarus was raised to life. This is simply because Jesus is not the author of death, but of life and He gives everlasting life. God punished man when he transgressed God's command and from then onward the death reigned.

The death reigned from Adam to Moses even when there was no written law because man was under the dispensation of Conscience. Satan cannot take the life of anyone who is righteous before God. Satan asked permission to end the life of Job but God denied permission to Satan while at the same time God granted him power to torment Job.

 "And the LORD said unto Satan, Behold, he is in thine hand; but save his life". (Job 2:6)

As per the prophecy in Genesis 3:15, which says God has put enmity between the serpent and the woman, the serpent is given the power to bruise the heel of the seed of the woman but then the seed of the woman is given the power to bruise the head of Satan. This prophecy is about Jesus bruising the head of Satan and, indeed, Lord Jesus Christ defeated Satan at the Cross.

OUR HOPE IS IN JESUS

Instead of taking on him the nature of angels, Jesus took on him the form of servant in the likeness of man, of the seed of Abraham and of David, in order that he might destroy the power of death, which is the devil. The death, which had sting to hurt men and the sin that caused death, which reigned from Adam to Moses, and would have continued if Jesus did not die for the salvation of men, was defeated at the cross.

The devil is defeated and the power of death is destroyed, thus rendering Satan with no power over believers in Christ. In the death and resurrection of Jesus there was a way made for the deliverance of them that were subject to the fear of death in their entire lifetime.

"Forasmuch then as the children are partakers of flesh and blood, he also himself likewise took part of the same; that through death he might destroy him that had the power of death, that is, the devil; and deliver them who through fear of death were all their lifetime subject to bondage. For verily he took not on him the nature of angels; but he took on him the seed of Abraham". (Hebrews 2:14-16)

As Jesus had promised He laid down His life for the sake of sinners that they may believe in Him and be saved and He took it back in His resurrection. In Revelation 1:18 Jesus said...

"I am he that live, and was dead; and, behold, I am alive for evermore, Amen; and have the keys of hell and of death"

Jesus holds the key to the hell and death and no one can put any one in hell or subject one to death without the permission from Lord Jesus Christ, who holds the key to the hell and death.

God did not create any one to die. Causing death was not His purpose but He punished mankind with death for sinning. It is by transgression of God's command that man was punished unto death.

Satan cannot end the life of a believer in Christ and the life of a believer in Christ does not end at any time, but it continues beyond the death. The death is only a temporary transition from earthly life to eternal life for a believer in Christ and the believer in Christ lives for ever and ever with Lord Jesus Christ.

The death is cessation of this earthly life and a fully unconscious state for an unbeliever in Christ until he is resurrected at the end for judgment and damnation in 'lake of fire' for ever and ever. Death of believer should not be compared with that of unbeliever to say that the death is cessation of life for all.

The first evidence that the soul of a believer in Christ shall not lie dead in the grave is seen in the words of none other than our Savior Lord Jesus Christ, who said to the repentant thief that he will be with the Lord in paradise the same day.

The prophecy of crucifixion of Jesus and that he will be numbered along with two transgressors was recorded in Isaiah 53:12. Rightly so, when Jesus was crucified two thieves were also crucified on his either side. While one of the two thieves mocked Jesus another prayed to Jesus to remember him when He comes in His kingdom but the thief who repented before the Lord he was promised of his presence with the Lord Himself.

"And Jesus said unto him, Verily I say unto thee, Today shalt thou be with me in paradise". (Luke 23:43)

Apostle Paul wrote that when our bodies groan and are laid to be decayed in the dust our soul will be with the Lord and at the first resurrection we will rise to meet the Lord in the air. It is this great hope that a believer in Christ has that his soul will not perish but will be with the Lord Jesus Christ for ever and ever.

"For we know that if our earthly house of this tabernacle were dissolved, we have a building of God, and house not made with hands, eternal in the heavens" (2 Corinthians 5:1)

 "We are confident, I say, and willing rather to be absent from the body, and to be present with the Lord". (2 Corinthians 5:8)

Those believers in Christ who have gone before us will rise first to be with the Lord for ever and ever and those that are alive when the Lord shall come with a shout, with the voice of the archangel, and with the trump of God, will be caught up to meet the Lord in the air to be with Him for ever and ever. The sinner will rise to be judged and condemned and will be cast into 'lake of fire' along with Satan and his fallen angels where there is gnashing of teeth and torment for ever and ever.

 "For the Lord himself shall descend from heaven with a shout, with the voice of the archangel, and with the trump of God: and the dead in Christ shall rise first: Then we which are alive and remain shall be caught up together with them in the clouds, to meet the Lord in the air: and so shall we ever be with the Lord". (1 Thessalonians 4:16-17)

QUEST FOR KNOWLEDGE ON DEATH

Man has an unflinching curiosity to know about the power of death, the death, and the life after death. There are many myths about the death and even among Christians there are differing views. Bible gives a believer in Christ great comfort that he or she will be with the Lord for ever and ever after death.

The life after death for believers is extremely pleasant and good according to Scriptures and, therefore, a believer in Christ does not need to be afraid of death. Lord Jesus Christ defeated the power of death and the death once and for all by His own resurrection.

The grave could not hold Him and He resurrected without seeing any corruption of His body. Jesus said He had the power to lay down His life and take it back at his own discretion and He did so. Lord Jesus Christ also assured his followers that they need not be afraid of death because He gives them everlasting life.

According to Bible Lord Jesus Christ is the only one who has the authority to pardon sins of a person, and salvation is by grace through faith in Him. Jesus is the Son of God, and the very God Himself. Jesus became one like us and came to this earth, lived like a man among us.

Jesus was fully divine and fully human and this truth is very hard to understand by an unbeliever. Jesus died, rose on the third day and ascended into heaven. He is seated at the right hand of the Father highly exalted. He is given the name above all names and every knee shall bow to Him. Jesus will come again soon.

The Scripture says that we shall not all sleep, but we shall all be changed. When Lazarus was dead for four days Jesus saw him and said "Our friend Lazarus sleeps..." The disciples of Jesus took his saying at face value and thought Lazarus was, indeed, sleeping.

However, Jesus spoke of the death of Lazarus and said he is dead. Jesus said that He will wake him up from his sleep, indicating that He will raise Lazarus. Martha believed and said to Jesus that she knew Lazarus would rise in the resurrection at the last day. But then, Jesus said He is the resurrection. (cf. John: 11:13, 14, 24, and 25)

"Jesus said unto her, I am the resurrection, and the life: he that believeth in me, though he were dead, yet shall he live" (John 11:25)

MARY DID NOT RECOGNIZE JESUS

It is interesting that the Peter and John disciples of Lord Jesus Christ did not take it serious that there was scripture saying that He will rise again. Mary Magdalene did not recognize Lord Jesus Christ until He called her by name.

"And said unto them, Thus it is written, and thus it behooved Christ to suffer, and to rise from the dead the third day" (Luke 24:46)

The narration of the resurrection of our Lord Jesus Christ is marvelously described in John Chapter 20. On the first day of the week Mary Magdalene went to the sepulcher and saw that stone was taken away from the sepulcher. She was surprised to see that there was no stone laid on the sepulcher.

Before Jesus was buried the chief priests and Pharisees went to Pilate and said to him that Jesus had told that He will rise again in three days, and, therefore, a command be issued that the sepulcher be secured well until the third day, in order that the disciples of Jesus may not go and steal the body and say that He rose from the dead.

Pilate agreed to their suggestion and said to them to have watch and make it secure as they can. The chief priests and Pharisees, therefore, went and made sure that the sepulcher was secured with the seal on the stone and setting a watch. (cf. Matthew 27:62-66) From Matthew 15:47 and Matthew 27:56 it can be seen there Mary Magdalene, was not the Mary the mother of Jesus. There were several women by the name "Mary" but here the name of Mary Magdalene is mentioned.

Mary Magdalene was the woman out of whom seven devils were cast out and she was healed of evil spirits and infirmities. And certain women, which had been healed of evil spirits and infirmities, Mary called Magdalene, out of whom went seven devils, (Luke 8:2) Mary Magdalene ran to Simon Peter, and the other disciple (John), whom Jesus loved, and said to them that "they have taken away the Lord out of the sepulcher and we not where they have laid Him".

Mary Magdalene was the first to reach the sepulcher but there were other women also with her. Other women were Mary the mother of James, and Salome. (Cf. Mark 16:1 and Matthew 28:1) Peter and John ran to the sepulcher but John outran Peter and reached the Sepulcher.

John stooped down and looked in and saw linen clothes lying but he did not go in. Peter came following came in and went into the sepulcher and saw that linen lie there. Importantly the napkin that was wrapped around the body of Lord Jesus was not along with the linen clothes but it was found wrapped together in a place by itself.

From John 11:44 it is understood that there was napkin around the face of Lazarus whom Lord Jesus resurrected. Here we see the napkin was not along with linen but it was found in a place by itself. Then John also went into the sepulcher and saw and believed they Lord Jesus Christ rose from the dead.

Surprisingly, even though they were disciple of Lord Jesus Christ they did not know that there was scripture saying that he must rise again from the dead. There were two scriptures according to which Lord Jesus Christ should rise from the dead.

"Ought not Christ to have suffered these things, and to enter into his glory?" (Luke 24:26)

"And said unto them, Thus it is written, and thus it behooved Christ to suffer, and to rise from the dead the third day" (Luke 24:46).

CHRIST'S BODY AFTER RESURRECTION

"For as yet they knew not the scripture that he must rise again from the dead. Then the disciples went away again unto their own home" (John 20:9-10)

The disciples of Lord Jesus Christ went home but Mary stood outside the sepulcher and wept. She stooped down and looked into the sepulcher and saw two angels in white sitting. One angel was sat at the head and the other at feet where the body of Lord Jesus Christ was laid. The angels inquired Mary as to why she was weeping and she said to the angels that they have taken away Her Lord, and she did not know where they have laid Him.

Immediately she turned back and saw Lord Jesus Christ standing but she did not recognize Him. She thought she saw gardener and asked Him if He had taken away the body of Lord Jesus Christ, and if so, she would take the body away. Lord Jesus Christ called her by name and Mary recognized Him and called Him as "Master "Mary Magdalene recognized Lord Jesus Christ only after He called her by name. She responded by saying "Rabboni" which is to say "Master".

The Lord said to her not to touch her because He did not ascend unto the Father. There are some interpretations contradictory to each other about Lord Jesus Christ asking her not to touch Him. The simplest explanation is that she should not cling to her as an obstruction to Him nor she should stop at that but to go ahead and tell His disciples about His resurrection and that He will ascend unto the Father.

Mary Magdalene went to the disciples of Lord Jesus Christ and told them that she saw Lord Jesus Christ and about the instructions the Lord gave to her. It was the first day of the week and on the same evening the disciples assembled with the doors shut because they feared Jews. Lord Jesus Christ came into their midst even when the doors remain shut and said to them "Peace be unto you".

After this He showed His hands which were nailed and His body which was scourged. The disciples saw Lord Jesus Christ and were glad. Lord Jesus Christ said to them once again "Peace be unto you"

LORD JESUS APPEARD TO THOMAS

Lord Jesus Christ commissioned them to proclaim the Gospel and said to them just as the Father sent Him with a mission He was also sending His disciples with a mission and He breathed on them saying "Receive you the Holy Ghost".

Later in Acts Chapter 1 it is recorded that that they should wait at Jerusalem and they should start on their mission only after the Holy Ghost had come upon them. No one except God only can forgive any one's sins and there should not be any misunderstanding about Lord saying to them that whosoever sins they remit they are remitted and whosoever sins they retain shall be retained.

Each individual is responsible for his/her own sins and only when they repent of their sins they receive salvation. Lord Jesus

Christ's words were in relation to the building of the Church. Thomas Didymus was not with them when Lord Jesus Christ appeared to the disciples when the doors were shut and He breathed on them the Holy Spirit.

When other disciples said to them they saw the Lord Thomas said to them that unless he sees Lord Jesus Christ personally and see in his hands nail marks and put his finger into the print marks of the nails and his side he would not believe. After eight days again when the disciples were in closed doors Thomas was also with them.

Lord Jesus Christ came into their midst, even the second time, when the doors were shut and said "Peace be unto you". Lord Jesus Christ said to Thomas to put his finger into His hands and His side to make sure that He was Lord Jesus Christ and also admonished him that he should not be faithless but be a believer in Him.

Thomas answered and said "My Lord and my God". Lord Jesus Christ did many miracles and they are not all recorded, but only those which are enough to prove that He was the Son of God and by believing they may have life through His name.

"I will declare the decree: the LORD hath said unto me, Thou art my Son\; this day have I begotten thee" (Psalms 2:7)

"Therefore my heart is glad, and my glory rejoices: my flesh also shall rest in hope. For thou wilt not leave my soul in hell\; neither wilt thou suffer thine Holy One to see corruption" (Psalms 16:9-10)

THE LORD IS ALWAYSS WITH US

"Go ye therefore, and teach all nations, baptizing them in the name of the Father, and of the Son, and of the Holy Ghost:

Teaching them to observe all things whatsoever I have commanded you: and, lo, I am with you always, [even] unto the end of the world. Amen" (Matthew 28:19-20)

Thomas Didymus, who was one of the disciples of Lord Jesus Christ, was not present along with the other disciples when they assembled together at one place because of the fear of Jews. When Lord Jesus Christ appeared to them even when the doors were shut He removed their fear from them and said unto them "Peace be unto you".

The Lord gave His peace to them. His peace was not as the world gave but it was that peace soothes the hearts of those who receive it and it is everlasting. The peace that the Lord gives to us infuses courage in us who trust Him as the Lord. It was at a different time period when the disciples told Thomas that they saw the Lord. The conversation among the disciples of Lord Jesus Christ is interesting.

The disciples of Lord Jesus Christ who saw Him gave testimony that they saw Him, but Thomas was not convinced with their testimony and surely desired to see Him and believe that He is the Lord. He desired to place finger in the print marks of the nails in the hands of Jesus Christ and thrust his hands into the side of the Lord.

It was after eight days when all the disciples and this time including Thomas assembled together Lord Jesus Christ appeared to them second time and said to them "Peace be unto you". It is very noteworthy that Thomas did not ask Lord Jesus Christ directly to show His hands in order that he may thrust his finger into the nail-marks in His hands and thrust his hand into the side of the Lord, but it was Lord Jesus Christ, who voluntarily offered to show to Thomas Didymus and called him by his name.

The Lord said to him that he may do what he desired to do to be sure of the fact that he saw the Lord. Obviously the disciples did not know that the Lord heard the disciples when they spoke to Thomas that they saw the Lord. Their testimony about Lord Jesus Christ was not in the same place where they assembled earlier but it was outside the place.

Thomas was not present when they assembled earlier and now he was with them when the disciples gave testimony about the Lord. With all the disciples including Thomas Didymus assembled the Lord appeared to them again and said to them second time "Peace be unto you".

It was this time that the Lord Himself said to Thomas to put his finger into His hands and His side that he may believe that He was the Lord. It was even before Thomas asked the Lord to show his hands and his side that the Lord Himself offered his hands and side to Thomas to peruse and believe.

The Lord was with them first time and until he said "Peace be unto you" they did not recognize Him. Thomas did not recognize the Lord until he placed his fingers into the nail-marks of Lord Jesus and thrust his hand into His side. The Lord was with all of them when they were conversing with one another outside but they did not see the Lord. The Lord heard their conversation but they knew not that the Lord heard them speak to one another. The Lord offered voluntarily to Thomas His hands and side to be perused that he may believe that He was their Lord and Savior. Thomas believed and called out loudly "My Lord and my God. The Lord is always with us even if we do not see Him physically. ;

RESURRECTED BODY

And he said unto them, Cast the net on the right side of the ship, and ye shall find. They cast therefore, and now they were not able to draw it for the multitude of fishes" (John 21:6) After Thomas was convinced of his question about resurrection of Lord Jesus Christ

Lord Jesus showed Himself again to the disciples at the sea of Tiberius. His appearance was not before Simon Peter and Thomas, Nathanael and sons of Zebedee and two other disciples decided to turn to their own professions because they were still unsure about the resurrection of Lord Jesus Christ. It all appeared, perhaps, as fable to them that in spite of seeing Lord Jesus Christ little while ago they decided to return to their own professions.

Simon Peter said "I go a fishing" and the rest of the disciples concurred with him and said that they also will follow him. As they turned to their profession according to their own choice and will they caught not even a single fish the entire night even though they were professional fishers. Early in the morning desperate as they were with no yield Lord Jesus stood on the shore and yet the disciples did not recognize Him.

It is strange that even though the Lord appeared to them little while ago to Peter and other disciples except Thomas when they were assembled even when the doors were shut and said to them "Peace be unto you" and then later when Thomas was present in their midst after eight days Jesus appeared to them even when the doors were shut and yet they did not recognize Him this time at the shore. Lord Jesus Christ asked them "Children have ye any meat?" and they answered "No".

Jesus said to them to cast the net on the right side of the ship and assured them they shall find the fish. They took His suggestion and cast their net on the right side of their ship and the catch was so great that they could not draw the net out because of the multitude of the fishes in the net. At this point John recognized Lord Jesus Christ and said to Simon Peter that it was Lord Jesus Christ who stood on the shore and asked them to cast the net on the right side of the ship. Simon Peter heard from John about Lord Jesus Christ and he jumped into the sea after girding himself with fisher's coat because he was naked until then.

The simplicity of Peter is adorable\; nonetheless he was quick in actions. Simon Peter was a fisherman who followed Lord Jesus Christ from the time he was called and yet he did not recognize the risen Lord Jesus Christ. He thought of walking on water when he saw Jesus walking on water because he stumbled in faith he started sinking.

However, when he called out to Lord Jesus Christ in faith to save him, the Lord responded immediately and pulled him out of the water to safety. When Jesus was about to be crucified he said, inadvertently, such a thing may not happen to him but the Lord said to him to get behind him because he was harboring evil thoughts.

The purpose of Jesus coming into this world was to fulfill the will of the Father and to bruised for our sins and Peter did not know that purpose. Peter pulled out his sword and cut the ear of one of the soldiers when they were arresting Jesus but the Lord said to him that he who strives to live by the sword will die by the sword and he healed the soldier with restoring his ear. Peter denied Jesus three times but repented later.

In his life Simon Peter stood as a great testimony for Lord Jesus Christ and history says that he was crucified upside down according to his voluntary disposition in consequence of the persecution he faced for standing for Him. Jesus was crucified on the cross and was buried and he rose from the dead with uncorrupted body in His glorified body on the third day.

It is so comforting to note that we will also rise with glorified bodies at the resurrection when out Lord Jesus Christ returns. "But some man will say, how are the dead raised up? And with what body do they come? Thou fool, that which thou sowest is not quickened, except it die: And that which thou sowest, thou sowest not that body that shall be, but bare grain, it may chance of wheat, or of some other grain" (1 Corinthians 15:35-37)

CHAPTER 31

THE MYSTERY OF RESURRECTION

Behold, I shew you a mystery; we shall not all sleep, but we shall all be changed,   in a moment, in the twinkling of an eye, at the last trump: for the trumpet shall sound, and the dead shall be raised incorruptible, and we shall be changed. 1 Corinthians 15:51-52

"Thou fool, that which thou sowest is not quickened, except it die" 1 Corinthians 15:36

Concerning the resurrection and resurrected body Apostle Paul explains in 1 Corinthians 15:35-58

There would be many questions as to how the dead are raised and what their bodies look like when they are raised from the dead. A seed that is sown in the ground should die first before it comes up with a quickened body.

The seed sown in the ground, whether it be of wheat or some other grain, is not sown as a full-grown body but it is sown as a seed. It is God who gives the seed a body that pleases Him and every seed comes up with a different body that God gives it.

A butterfly, before it undergoes metamorphosis, would be like a worm; but when it becomes a butterfly it is so beautiful. The flesh of man differs from that of the flesh of animals, fish and birds. Some bodies are terrestrial, and some celestial and these differ from one another. God has also placed celestial bodies in the galaxy. The Sun, the moon, the stars differ from one another and each star differs in glory from the other.

So is the resurrected body of the dead. The body is sown in corruption, dishonor, and in weakness but when it is raised it is raised in incorruption, glory, and in power.

The natural body dies and is raised in spiritual body. The resurrected body has the likeness of natural body and spiritual body similar to the one of risen Lord, who could suddenly appear and disappear at a place where He desired to go and even passing the shut doors and also could eat fish.

The first man Adam was made a living soul when God breathed His spirit into his nostrils and the last Adam, who is our Lord Jesus Christ, became a quickening spirit. The first man was not spiritual but had a fleshly natural body but the resurrected body is spiritual.

God created man in His own image in the likeness of the triune God. (Genesis 1:26-27).

God created man out of dust and man returns to dust when he dies. The death came into this world as a result of sin and Lord Jesus Christ was triumphant over death.

Man belongs to earth but Lord Jesus Christ was from heaven. The body which is created from the earth belongs to earth and the body that is from heaven belongs to heaven. Flesh and blood cannot inherit the kingdom of God.

The natural body needs to necessarily die to acquire heavenly body. Corrupted body cannot inherit incorruption. The resurrection and resurrected body was a mystery for long but is revealed unto us.

We have a fair idea about the attributes of resurrected body and we will have a change in the twinkling of an eye at the last trump when Lord Jesus Christ comes in clouds with the shout of an archangel and we are caught up to meet Him in the air to be with Him for ever and ever.

There is no dearth of people in the world, suffering pain and sickness as a consequence of their willful acts of committing sin. Some, who have enjoyed pleasures of the world, get enlightened after watching others suffer. They make known to others their learning about suffering. Those, who are learning from the errors eventually teach others to be careful.

Except for the one, who is born of Virgin Mary, when the power of the Holy Spirit overshadowed her, and, thus is sinless, and thereafter lived a life without any blemish and sin, no one else deserves worship.

The only one, who is the Son of God, Lord Jesus Christ, is sinless, and without any blemish. The Lord, who has not committed any sin, and who was set apart for our salvation, and as a mediator between God and man alone is worthy to receive worship.

It may be noted that those who get enlightened after watching others suffer, and come forth with advices, are not gods and surely they do not deserve worship.

The Lord became a perfect sacrifice on behalf sinners. He became sin for us and died on the cross. Our sin was judged on the cross. He offered His own body and blood for the remission of sins. Salvation is available to all those who confess that "Jesus is Lord", and believe in heart that God raised him from the dead, will be saved.

"That if thou shalt confess with thy mouth the Lord Jesus, and shalt believe in thine heart that God hath raised him from the dead, thou shalt be saved. For with the heart man believeth unto righteousness; and with the mouth confession is made unto salvation" (Romans 10:9-10)

"For the Lord himself shall descend from heaven with a shout, with the voice of the archangel, and with the trump of God: and the dead in Christ shall rise first: Then we which are alive [and] remain shall be caught up together with them in the clouds, to meet the Lord in the air: and so shall we ever be with the Lord" 1 Thessalonians 4:16-17

"O death, where [is] thy sting? O grave, where [is] thy victory? The sting of death is sin; and the strength of sin is the law. But thanks [be] to God, which giveth us the victory through our Lord Jesus Christ". (1 Corinthians 15:55-57)

www.ingramcontent.com/pod-product-compliance
Lightning Source LLC
Chambersburg PA
CBHW061724020426
42331CB00006B/1085